Louis I. Kahn

LOUIS I. KAHN

by
Romaldo Giurgola
Jaimini Mehta

Westview Press
Boulder, Colorado

First published in 1975 in Zürich, Switzerland
by Verlag für Architektur Artemis
Zürich und München.

Published in 1975 in the United States of America
by Westview Press, Inc.
1898 Flatiron Court
Boulder, Colorado 80301
Frederick A. Praeger, Publisher and Editorial Director.

Library of Congress Cataloging in Publication Data

Giurgola, Romaldo and Mehta, Jaimini
    Louis I. Kahn.

    Includes index.
    1. Kahn, Louis I., 1901–1974.
Na737.K32G58   720'.92'4   75–19210
ISBN 0-89158-502-8

Printed and bound in Zürich, Switzerland.

An Homage to Louis I. Kahn (1901-1974) by Jonas Salk

Out of the mind of a tiny whimsical man
who happened by chance,
great forms have come,
great structures, great spaces that function.
Some houses the essence of the past,
others the creators, the discoverers and leaders
of an emerging future.
The wonder surrounding it all
is in the mystery
of his existence
and in his creations,
a mystery that will endure.

For five decades he prepared himself
and did in two
what others wish they could do in five.
How did he sense
what he seemed to know about Nature
to reveal
in form and in function
eternal truths and beauty
each the verification of the other —
From whence came
his originality,
his boldness,
his courage —

What, or where, was the source
of his inspiration,
of his judgment —
There will be found
the creative process
of Nature itself.

How does one capture and convey
the essence of a living being
whose words were those of a poet,
whose cadence that of a musician,
who had the vision of an artist,
the understanding of a philosopher,
the knowledge of a metaphysician,
the reason of a logician —

What he caused to appear
out of the invisible and the intangible
allows us to see and to touch
the fruits of creation that continues without end
as if without beginning.
What we see is not simply
discovery of what heretofore existed,
nor restatement of old perceptions.
He brought to view a new reality.

It is not without cause
that our thoughts are
of essence,
of life,
of continuous creation
because we speak
of one touched by the divine spark;
one marked to reveal that
among men
some are possessed
by a creative and constructive power
to balance
the power to destroy.

The greatness of any age
is in the works
of those whose traces endure.
We are gathered
to pay homage and respect
to a man whose imagination
and whose work
will have marked the time in which we live.

Our feelings of pride
are mixed with feelings of regret
that it will never be known
how much, nor what more,
would have been expressed
had life lingered
until the capacity to create began to ebb.

It is our good fortune
to have known him,
worked with him,
loved him.
Nothing need be proffered
of what he has done
for his works and their affect
speak with more eloquence
than can otherwise be said.
For him to be taken
at the flood of the tide
leaves us engulfed in sadness.

As if drawn by some force
to give expression to the meaning
of the unmeasurable dimension of relationship

our paths crossed
allowing each to help the other
to say and to reveal
what would otherwise have been
unknowable.
He will speak no more
but the dialogue will go on.

He communicated what he comprehended.
One could understand
but never for him say
what he alone could convey.
Try, however you can,
to imagine yourself in his presence;
although the voice is mine
the words you will now hear are his.

From "Perspecta" 3, 1955

Order is . . .
Design is form-making in order.
Form emerges out of a system of construction.
Growth is a construction.
In order is creative force.
In design is the means — where, with what, when, with
how much?
The nature of space reflects what it wants to be.
Is the auditorium a Stradivarius
or is it an ear?
Is the auditorium a creative instrument
keyed to Bach or Bartok
played by the conductor
or is it a convention hall?
In the nature of space is the spirit and the will to exist
in a certain way.
Design must closely follow that will.
Therefore a stripe painted horse is not a zebra.
Before a railroad station is a building
it wants to be a street,
it grows out of the needs of street
out of the order of movement
a meeting of contours englazed.
Thru the nature — why?
Thru the order — what?
Thru design — how?
A Form emerges from the structural elements inherent in
the form.
A dome is not conceived when questions arise how to
build it.
Nervi grows an arch,
Fuller grows a dome.
Mozart's compositions are designs.

9

They are exercises of order — intuitive.
Design encourages more designs.
Designs derive their imagery from order.
Imagery is the memory — the Form.
Style is an adopted order.
The same order created the elephant and created man.
They are different designs,
begun from different aspirations,
shaped from different circumstances.
Order does not imply Beauty.
The same order created the dwarf and Adonis.
Design is not making Beauty.
Beauty emerges from selection,
affinities,
integration,
love.
Art is a form making life in order — psychic
order is intangible:
It is a level of creative consciousness
forever becoming higher in level.
The higher the order the more diversity in design.
Order supports integration.
From what the space wants to be the unfamiliar may be
revealed to the architect.
From order he will derive creative force and power of
self-criticism
to give form to this unfamiliar.
Beauty will evolve.

And so will Lou Kahn's creations, across time,
as the unfamiliar becomes familiar,
revealing "the fullness of his symphonic composing."

And, for all this
Thank you
Lou.

University of Pennsylvania
Philadelphia
Memorial Convocation
2 April 1974

Introduction

This is a book about architecture — as much about architecture as it is about the architecture of Louis Kahn, for the work of Louis Kahn is above all a constant search for the very nature of architecture. The work presented here — both architectural and philosophical — is a manifestation of this search for the fundamentals. It is also a vehicle of communication to other architects — communication of an attitude which not only raises questions about the nature of architecture that we have taken for granted for so long, but which also points towards new horizons.

In approaching a highly complex and essentially non-sequential thought, we have made a distinction between a more general and abstract philosophical vocabulary and the architectural one. While the architectural vocabulary is tangible and can be made evident through buildings and projects, such connection is not always obvious between the work and the philosophical thought. It is more like a set of general, philosophical attitudes which might guide all human endeavors, be it architecture or science or anything else. This philosophical vocabulary is presented here under four titles: 1) Silence and Light, 2) The Sense of Man, 3) The Sense of Place, and 4) The Institutions of Man. The architectural vocabulary is articulated in the chapter entitled "Architecture."

Our task is twofold: on the one hand we hope to restate possibly in new contexts what Kahn has said on numerous occasions in a very poetic and somewhat cryptic way; on the other hand, we hope to place his work within a historical and theoretical perspective by distinguishing between the circumstantial decisions and the fundamental attitudes that permeate his work. This is attempted in the chapters "The Universal and the Eternal" and "The Architect as a Person." None of this can be done, however, without a certain sense of humility. The very nature of the task involves simplifying for the purpose of communication that which is complex and non-categorical. This book, therefore, is conceived of as a kind of supplement to Kahn's own statement — to fill in the gaps that he, not having a scholarly inclination, has left open.

His own use of language — singularly free of slogans — is indicative of a mind which is not distracted by the simplicity of abstractions. For example, he cautions us against the temptation to seek a "theory of architecture" here. He told us, as fellow architects, "The distinctions I have made between 'measurable' and 'unmeasurable,' between 'form' and 'design,' or 'servant' and 'served spaces' are dichotomous distinctions made only to help thought. The mind knows that in reality these are all one — in fact, the mind is secretly looking for the oneness in them. They are not even limited to architecture alone; they are simply offered as the work of mind to further thought." It is for this reason that there is no obvious and methodological connection between the thought and the architecture.

We hope that the organization of the book will convey this dichotomous relationship between the architecture and the idea. Its two main elements, the written text and the work, are seen as complementary to each other. The text is not intended merely as an explanation or description of the work; likewise, the work is presented not only as illustrations of the ideas. And yet neither of these is totally independent of the other. The work is presented here in six topical "chapters": 1) The House, 2) The Place of Worship, 3) The Institutions, 4) The Place of

Well-Being, 5) The Place of Work, and 6) The City. This body of work is seen as manifestations of an attitude toward the places of man rather than the development of a certain stylistic and formal language. That attitude is constantly being tested, clarified, and strengthened by the work.

These "chapters" are placed alternately between those aspects of Kahn's work which deal with architecture in the most general way. While the manifestations themselves are highly personal, the thought belongs to the idea "architecture." Such a collage of the particular and the general, we hope, would lead the reader into an awareness of a perspective within which all individual work should be seen.

What is presented here, then, is simply a presentation — not answers, not formulas for action, and certainly not a theory. Louis Kahn is not a polemicist. He has a certain way of saying things, not because that is the only way of saying them but because that is the least categorical and, as he himself says, "in the hope that a better way of saying can be found." However, if his language is tentative, his belief in these ideas is unshakable.

Vocabulary and Imagery

Silence and Light

There is an aura of mystery around the work of Louis Kahn. This is so because his vocabulary, both formal and philosophical, is personal. It is this singular nature of his work which challenges comprehension. His own use of language, deeply poetic and non-sequential, may have something to do with this; but if the use of language is an indication of the working of a mind, it also suggests an order of things and events different from the one we have so far generally understood and accepted.

Our judgments on art have so far been guided by one of two prevalent attitudes. On the one hand art is seen as a cultural item independent of the urgency of the moment or the earthly realities of human life. On the other hand it is seen as valid only to the extent that it expresses the everyday realities of man. At the core of the debate is the antagonism between aesthetics and relevance. Every work of art is expected to answer to one or the other. The mystery surrounding the architecture of Kahn stems from the fact that his architecture is guided by different theoretical considerations than those professed by modern architecture. At the root of the difference lies his concept of "Order," which replaces both aesthetics and relevance.

Aesthetics as commonly understood is a category whereby beauty is a value of expression – it is either more or less beautiful – and which relies on the invariables of form as the instruments of expression. An aesthetic experience, from such a point of view, would be an awareness that there exists a link between emotions and objects which embodies the sublime and the harmonious in the universe. Thus, it follows that a knowledge of what is beautiful, sublime, or harmonious is a precondition in an aesthetic consciousness.

This interpretation of aesthetics has provided the criteria of judgment in art for so long that it hardly occurs to us to question its validity. However, if knowledge of beauty is a precondition, "knowledge" must precede the realization of certain values to be expressed. If this is so, then what is to be expressed must also have some determined or determinable qualities – an aesthetic content before it becomes an aesthetic form. But this is not true. As Kahn points out, if content has any aesthetic qualities, we know them – not before, but after the transformation has taken place. In other words, the realization of those values which have never been expressed before must precede knowledge. This realization, then, motivates art before any consideration of beauty.

And in this lies the clue to Kahn's architecture. His consciousness of "order" underlies his realization, not only of that which is not yet expressed, but it also accounts for his understanding that "nothing fits unless everything fits." However, the very attempt to explain "order" immediately runs into trouble since it belongs to that part of the human consciousness which is beyond experience or knowledge and, therefore, explanation. It is through art that order becomes manifest. Therefore, Kahn refers to silence as the beginning of art in the same way that André Malraux called art the "voices of silence", for only silence prevails before knowledge.

Order can only be sensed: it is a consciousness that there is a common bond among all beings, natural or man-made, organic or inorganic – a sense that somehow in the sum total of all the laws of nature (the knowledge of which has always eluded man) lies the force which may be the beginning of all that exists. Man does not "know" all the laws of nature. If he knew them, he would not need nature anymore; he would achieve immortality. The ultimate nature of matter may always remain beyond his comprehension and knowledge. But he is endowed with a "sense" of the prevalence of order — its aura. Realization that something belongs to the order of things precedes knowledge of its corporeal qualities.

This relationship between realization and knowledge can also be viewed in another way. Realization is a source of joy. This joy must come before an awareness of beauty which is corporeal. There is no work of art that is not done in joy, no matter how tragic or gruesome or ugly its subject matter. The corporeal elements which constitute its presence, the instruments of expression, come later, and their availability depends upon man's knowledge of the laws of nature at that time.

Thus, art constitutes a unity of that which is and that which is not yet. While the instruments — the forms, structures, laws, etc. — are part of the prevalent presence, what is expressed has never existed before. So, all things in history that came to be for the first time, having no examples to follow, such as the discovery of the wheel or the first successful airplane or Beethoven's Fifth Symphony, came into being because man realized that they belong to the all-encompassing order, and not because of any knowledge of their being beautiful.

We cannot, therefore, presume that aesthetic considerations exist at the beginning. The beginning of art is in silence. In that state of mind, all considerations of beauty, knowledge, or even morality are meaningless. All one has is a feeling of the eternal commonality.

But the sense of order is not merely an intuitive realiza-

Eternity is of two brothers. The one desires to be to express, the other desires to be to make: the one light non-luminous, the other light luminous.

The prevailing luminous groups to ignite a wild dance of flaming prevalence spending to the emergence of material.

tion of a value. It is also the first inkling, a hint, of the instruments with which it can be expressed. If the realization resides in silence, in the very depth of human consciousness, what constitutes its actual expression are the objects and phenomena surrounding us. For Kahn, "Light" represents this world of phenomena. It is not only an instrument of our perception of things, but the very source of matter itself. It represents nature with all her laws, known or unknown to us, by which all matter is bound together.

"All matter", Kahn says, "is spent light ... It is light when finished being light becomes material. In silence is the will to be to express, and in light the will to be to make: the two aspects of the spirit, one non-luminous and the other luminous. The luminous turns to a prevalence of luminous, and this prevalence turns to flame, and flame deteriorates into material, and material becomes means, the possibilities, the evidence. So therefore mountains are spent light, the streams are spent light, the air is spent light. You are spent light ... And the will to express and the will to make meet in a kind of threshold which you say are the inspirations."

To put it another way, Kahn imposes upon himself the discipline to use nature's materials in a way that nature would approve, to make that which nature cannot make without man. In architecture, as in all art, Kahn sees the man/nature dichotomy coming to a harmonious resolution. If his architecture has any aesthetic qualities, these are certainly not the causes of his choices of elements. These choices are guided by the intrinsic validities. Thus, by introducing a new vocabulary, Kahn has opened up the question of form and content in art for a thorough re-evaluation. In architecture, visual and aesthetic approaches, like moralistic and socialistic approaches, lead to dead ends, for they take into consideration only partial and contingent aspects of the discipline of architecture. In the architecture of Louis Kahn, many of the assumptions of modern architecture — the architecture that was involved either with formal evolution or realism — are rejected, and the responsibility for the present is accepted in a more fundamental sense. The resulting architecture is not easy as it is not based on generic improvisations, and its forms are not sweet; but it comes strong and strident as are all things that are said for the first time.

The House

1 Weiss House

2 Fleisher House

3 Morris House

4 Adler House

5 Fisher House

6 Esherick House

7 Eleanor Donnelly Erdman Hall
Dormitory
Bryn Mawr, Pennsylvania

8 Mill Creek Housing
Philadelphia, Pennsylvania

The House

Out of more than a dozen houses designed by Kahn, we have choosen six which are representative. They also show, in microcosm, some of the elements prevalent in all his buildings. In addition to these six, this section also contains the public housing project in Philadelphia and the Erdman Hall Dormitory in Bryn Mawr.

Six projects presented on the same scale.

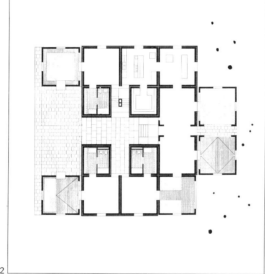

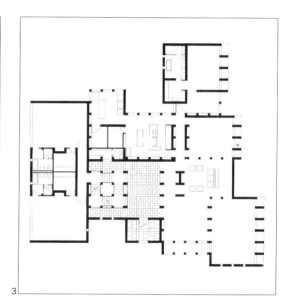

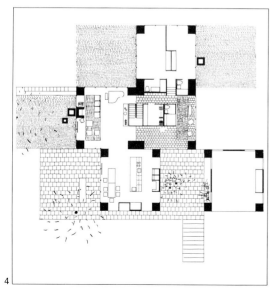

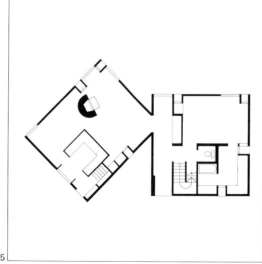

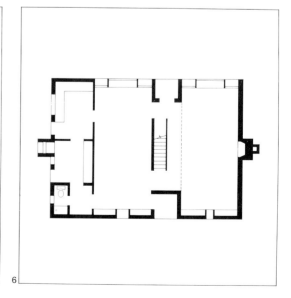

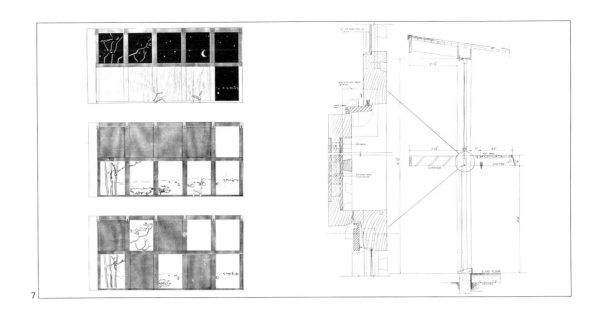

8

1 Weiss House.
2 Fleisher House.
3 Morris House.
4 Adler House.
5 Fisher House.
6 Esherick House.

Control of light has been Kahn's preoccupation from the beginning. Three different solutions are tried in these houses. In the Weiss House (7), the wall of the living-room is made of panels that move vertically, depending upon the quality of light desired.

At the Morris House (8) the structure itself is designed to control the rhythm of light inside the house.

And at the Fleisher House (9), the control of light is attempted by the shape of the windows.

All these solutions were developed further in many later projects.

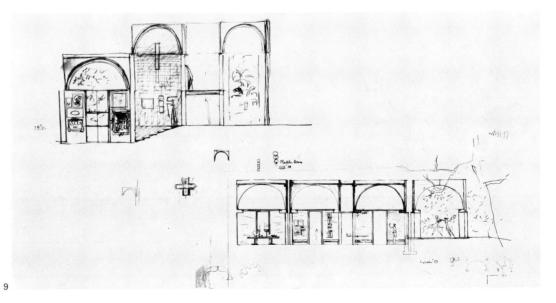

9

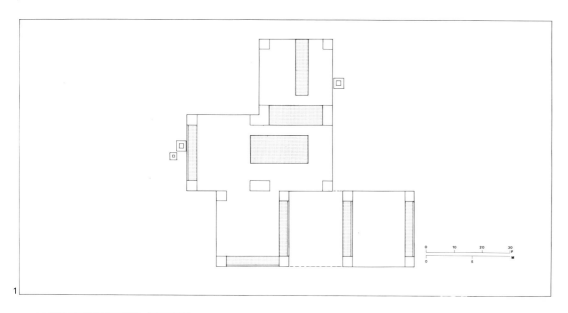

Organization of plan elements: At Adler House (1), the utilities ("servant spaces") are housed within the depth created by the structural elements, while at both Fisher House (2) and Esherick House (3), these are placed on the periphery.

1

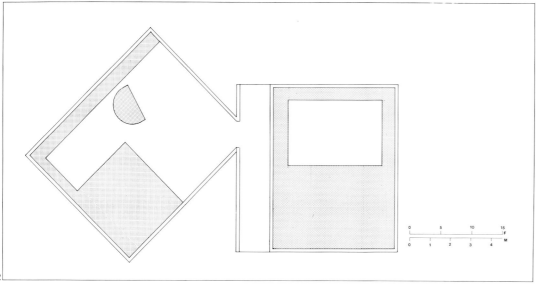

2

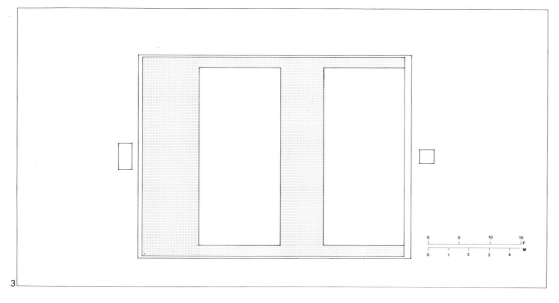

3

4 Weiss House. Exterior view.
5 Morris House. Model.
6 Esherick House. View from street.
7 Esherick House. Garden view.
8 Fisher House.
9 Fisher House. Entrance.

4

5

6

7

8

9

21

Fisher House. Exterior detail.

Fisher House. Corner window of living-room.

7 Eleanor Donnelly Erdman Hall Dormitory
Bryn Mawr, Pennsylvania

1960–1965

The building sits at the end of a suburban campus of a college for girls.

The dormitory is conceived as a large house for approximately 150 girls. The plan is structured by three halls defined by large hoods, which rise above the roof to bring in natural light. The "walls" of these halls contain the "servant" spaces. The individual rooms for the students make up the periphery of each of the three squares. Connections are achieved at the corners.

Construction consists of reinforced concrete frame with cinder block walls covered with slate on the exterior and plaster inside.

Exterior view as seen from the street.

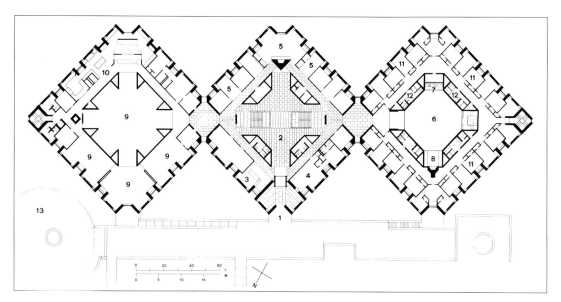

Plan.

1 Entree
2 Hall
3 Reception
4 Office
5 Visitors
6 Living-room
7 Pantry
8 Fire-place
9 Dining
10 Kitchen
11 Students' room
12 Toilets
13 Parking

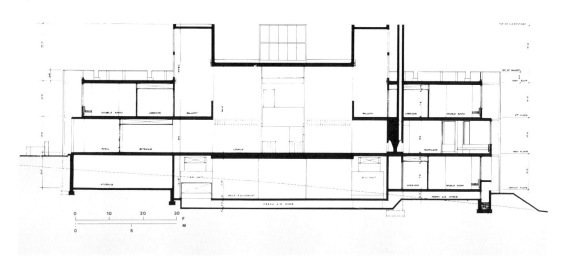

Cross section.

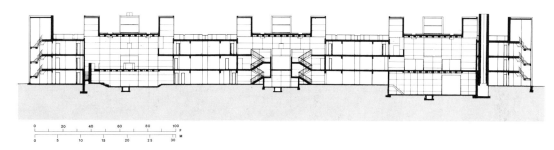

Longitudinal section.

A series of sketches showing the development of plan ▷ form. Note the interlocking rooms were a theme present from the earliest stages.

24

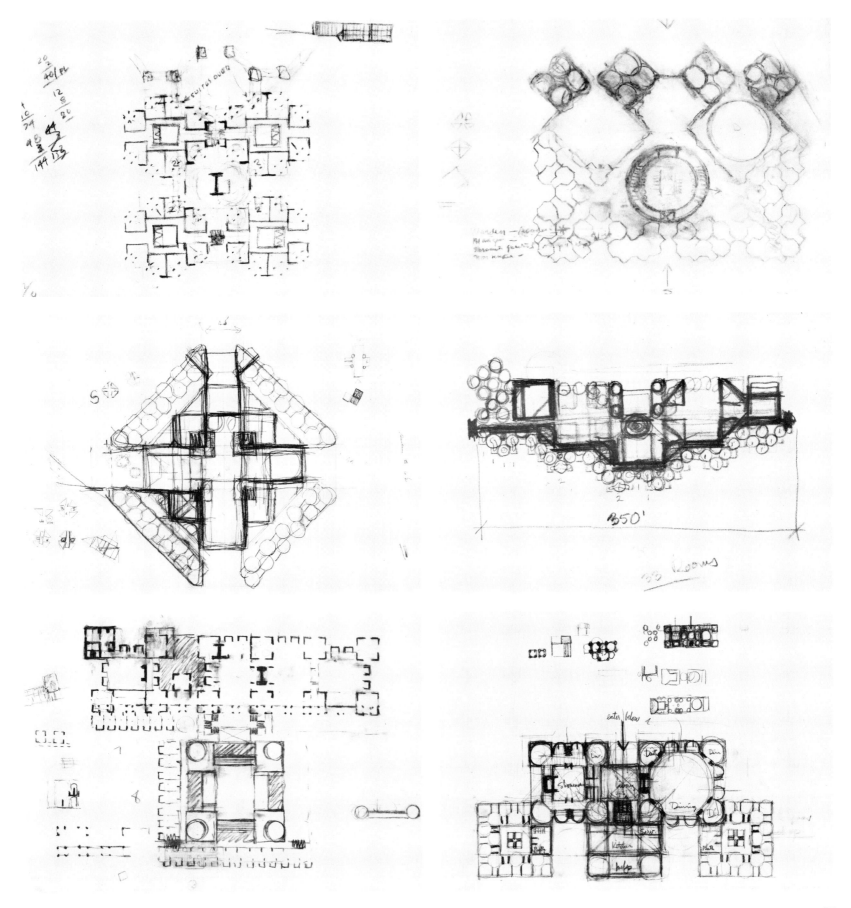

Living-room – view from the entrance hall.

8 Mill Creek Housing
Philadelphia, Pennsylvania

Group 1: 1952–1953
Group 2: 1959–1962

Kahn was commissioned to do this project in two parts. The first part consisted of the three towers and the semi-detached units around it and was designed in 1950, in association with Kenneth Day and Louis McAllister.

In 1959, Kahn designed the expansion west of the first project. This consisted of the row houses and the community building.

Construction is in the American vernacular. In the low buildings, walls made of brick and cinder blocks are load-bearing, while concrete is used to span openings. The towers are made with concrete frames and in-fill walls.

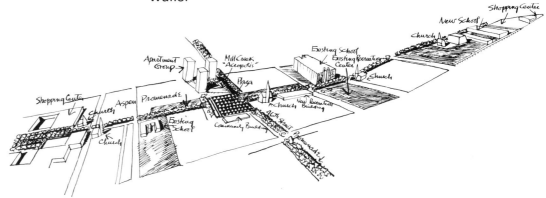

An early sketch shows that Kahn proposed a promenade connecting the housing project with surrounding institutions.

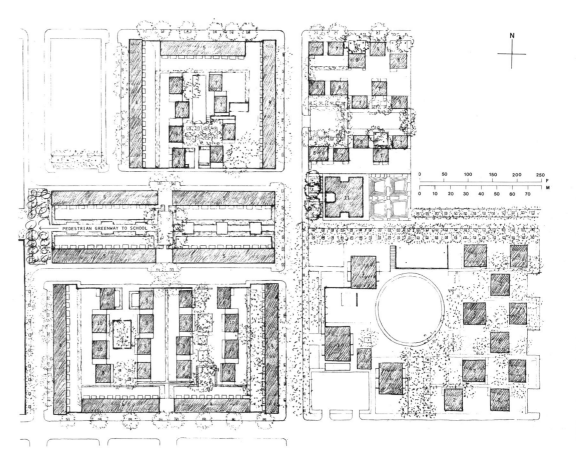

Site plan. Project 1, 1953.

1 16-story apartment building with 4 apartments/floor
2 2- or 3-story quad building (one house each quarter)
3 Mechanical building
4 2-story 2-bedroom row housing
5 2-story 3-bedroom row housing
6 2-story 1-bedroom twin house
7 2-story 2-bedroom twin house
8 2-story 3-bedroom twin house
9 3-story 4-bedroom twin house
10 3-story 5-bedroom twin house
11 Community building

Looking south-west. The view of the apartment towers.

A Typical floor-plan apartment tower.

1 Living-room
2 Kitchen
3 Bedroom
4 Bathroom
5 Terrace

B Plan Community building.

1 Entrance
2 Vestibule
3 Coats
4 Office
5 Meeting-room
6 Kitchen
7 Toilet

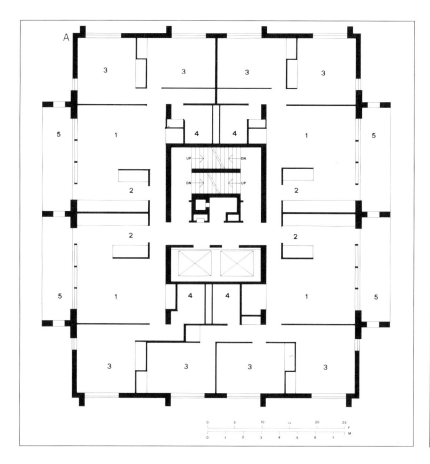

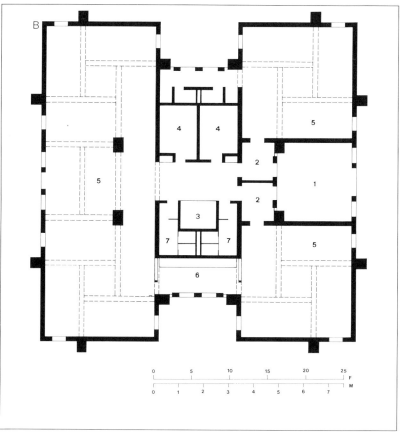

A typical court between 2-story quad buildings.

A   Upper-floor plan. 3-bedroom unit.
B   Lower-floor plan. 3-bedroom unit.
C/D 1-bedroom unit.
E/G Upper floor. 2-bedroom unit.
F/H Lower floor. 2-bedroom twins.
I/L Upper floor. 3-bedroom twins.
K/M Lower floor. 3-bedroom twins.

1 Living-room
2 Kitchen and dining
3 Bedroom
4 Bath
5 Storage
6 Garbage

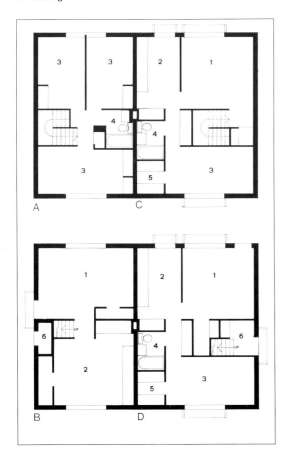

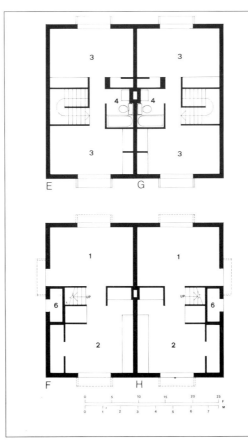

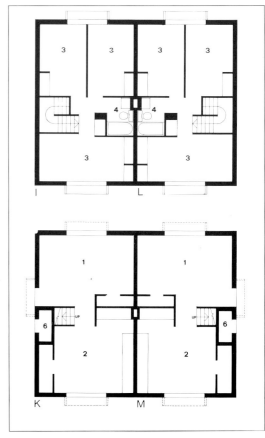

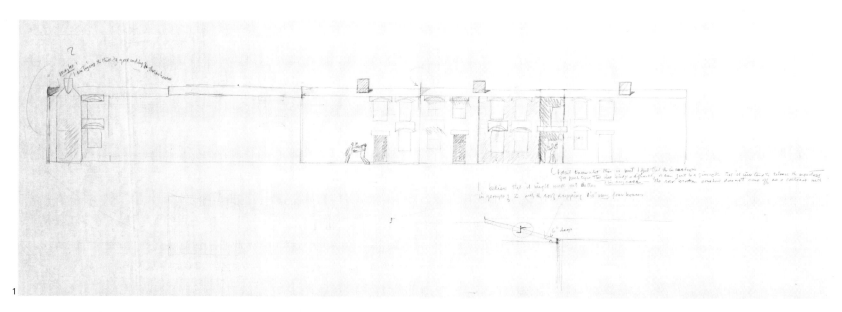

1

2

30

3

1/3 Two early elevation studies. The treatment of windows was not yet resolved.
2   Row houses facing the pedestrian greenway.
4   View looking west.

4

2- and 3-story twin houses view looking east.

The Sense of Man

Louis Kahn's singular understanding of the nature of architecture, as expressed through the metaphors of silence and light, is rooted in his unique perception of man. Here, he has realized those aspects of human nature which are not contingent upon history or the laws of evolution.

Our century is still dominated by the concept of man that we inherited from 19th century thought. It is a notion of man so closely linked to evolution and the meaning of man's existence to the future, that we seem to have lost track of the questions which may be central: If the root of mankind is man, then in what is the individual man himself rooted? Is there anything that is constant and transcendental in man? If we can answer these questions we will have found the beginnings of all human endeavors, whether architecture or scientific discovery or making a new fairy tale, for the beginning and the motivation for man's activity lies in the very root of man.

The search for this beginning has been a preoccupation of philosophers, but it has been assumed that the answers can be found in an intensive analysis of the human phenomena — the observable man. Since the Age of Enlightenment, everyone seeking to unravel the secrets of human endeavors has hoped to find it within the human phenomenon itself by applying to man the same scientific methods and tools so useful to measuring other natural phenomena. In attempting to articulate the motivations of man, Darwin, Freud, and Marx relied heavily on scientific methods.

We are indebted to Kahn for a re-evaluation of the problem of man. "Man is not nature but is made by nature."

The pregnancy of this statement becomes apparent once we distinguish between man the species and man the human.

Man the species is part of nature and, as such, is no different from any other species in nature. At this level man can be understood on the model of nature, like all physical phenomena subjected to the laws of nature. Unfortunately, man has been viewed only on this level, either as part of nature or as the master and controller of nature having reached a certain superiority through evolution. This partiality results from our quest for the "knowledge" of man — that is, to put everything about him in intellectually comprehensible categories. We have believed that, given the time and tools, we would ultimately acquire all there is to know about man. But only phenomena — physical phenomena — lend themselves to such a process of categorizing. It is applicable only to the measurable items of reality. It is obvious, therefore, that for the process of science to be applicable to the study of man, one must assume man to be a natural phenomenon, with qualities that can be studied in the same way and with the same tools as any other natural phenomenon. This has necessarily limited our concept of man.

Man the human, on the other hand, is beyond the reach of those instruments suitable for studying man the species. For such a study we will have to devise new tools, tools of introspection, for the humanness of man lies in his consciousness, in his silence. It is here that man differs from nature: nature does not have consciousness. What nature does is a happening without conscious effort. Thus the roots of man lie outside of nature, in his own consciousness, which is beyond time, space or circumstances. In other words, the humanness of man is not subject to cultural or evolutionary changes; neither is it subject to racial or ethnic differences between men.

The manifestations of his humanness occur in many ways. The way a man walks, talks, dresses or conducts himself all comes from his being a human. It is part of what Kahn calls the "will to be to express." This is to say that the reason for being is to express the nature of one's being; and, consciously or not, everything a man does is somehow tied to his desire to express the nature of his being. This is also to say that everyone deals with art in one way or another. Art is not limited only to the activity of consciously designing — the very act of being, in all its manifestations, is art. "Art," Kahn says, "is man's only real language since it strives to communicate in a way that reveals the 'human,' and that the 'will to be' in a man is really the 'will to be to express'."

Concepts such as "will" and "desire" do not really belong to the idea of man in the Greco-Christian tradition. In fact, it is inappropriate to speak of "will" or "desire" as concepts, since "concept" implies knowledge and, therefore, limits. Knowledge has boundaries — it is measurable. It can be understood in terms of more or less. A concept can be articulated and explained, but there is no way to explain or describe humanness. It can only be expressed.

"Desire" is the avenue of this expression. Again, to put it in Kahn's own words, "The three greatest desires of man are the desire to learn, desire to meet, and desire for well-being. They all serve, really, the will to be to express. This, you might say, is the reason for living." This is also a possible common denominator of all human activities. Can we say that all human activities, no matter what their immediate motivations may be, are ultimately rooted in these desires? Is this what the poets have termed "inspiration?"

"Desire to learn" is a motivation to find the commonality between all that is present. "In everything nature makes, there is a record of how it was made." This is to say that all natural phenomena display not only the processes of their making but also the primordial forces that determined the nature of their being. Similarly, in man lies the story of his humanness. The force that caused the "human" to emerge from the species is his "existence will," his undeniable demand to be human. Everything that comes into being in nature, either by natural forces or by the hands of man, has a similar "existence will." Man's desire to learn, then, comes from wanting somehow to sense this force. "All the institutions of man, whether they serve man's interest in medicine, or chemistry, or mechanics or architecture, are all ultimately answerable to this desire in man to find out what forces caused him to be and what means made it possible for him to be."

"Meeting" is both the essence and the source of the city. In other words, the city is an expression of man's desire to meet to express, to communicate. All the theoretical analyses of city — the sociological, economical, technological studies — all come down to the fact that the city began when the street was conceived as a place to meet. The street, Kahn says, is probably the first institution of man — "a meeting hall without a roof."

A city, after all, is built with overlapping networks of communication or exchange: exchange of ideas and information, exchange of goods, and, above all, exchange simply of people from one place to another to make all the other exchanges possible. Kahn is fond of suggesting that if we realize a store to be a meeting place between a customer and the storekeeper, we also visualize that even before any business is transacted, the first thing the storekeeper would do is serve coffee. Thus, in considering the architecture of this store, a place to welcome must be included as an inseparable element. This is what Kahn means by "form."

Once Kahn asked his students at the University of Pennsylvania to design "a place of well-being". This required first defining what one means by "a place of well-being" before translating it into a spatial configuration. It was one of the most self-searching experiences for everyone in the class; and though no two solutions were similar, there was a shared feeling at the end that such a "place," regardless of its size or purpose, is any place in which one feels a confirmation of the highest aspirations of man.

Such intangibles, which were discarded by modern architecture because they cannot be explained, guided the great architecture of the past and guides today the architecture of Kahn. "Nothing is important in the way of circumstances unless it conjures up all that is human." The realization of the pyramids or the Pantheon or the "first house that was built without any precedent whatsoever" belongs to man. These makings of man belong to the realm of things that nature cannot make without man. They did not just happen out of that constant movement of circumstances adjusting itself to the laws of nature. They came into being because man, motivated by his desire to express, first realized their existence and then asked nature to help him make them.

But desire needs structure. In itself, desire is irresponsible — it has a tendency to shoot in many directions and to cause disharmony. So expression really comes from desire which has been structured by thought — that is, by thoughtful choices. Kahn refers to this structuring element as "validity." It provides criteria for choices. As such, validity is a category of the intellect entering a process which begins in the realm of the unmeasurable and the undefinable of the human psyche.

Thus, from Kahn's realization of the humanness of man emerges the triad of human desire which, when helped by thought, leads to expression.

Validity is relative in character: what is valid for one situation may not be so for the next one. This relativity of validity is expressed by Kahn in his distinction between physical validity and psychological validity. The former has to do with the laws of nature, the way nature makes things. For example, it determines that the wheels of a wagon have to be round. This means that for man to make anything "in nature," it has to answer to the reality of nature.

Psychological validity, on the other hand, has to do with the reality of mind, which is different from the reality of nature. It gives courage to the painter to paint square wheels on a cannon to express the futility of war, and to the composer to write a symphony using only four notes. In Kahn's words: "Psychological validity is a sum total of attitudes in which you add to nature what nature cannot make without man."

The emphasis of desire is always toward the yet unrealized, that which is not yet invented but only sits in the consciousness as possible. Its validation comes from the way its own demands for presence meet the means which nature provides. In other words, it comes from man's making it the way nature would make it if she had the consciousness. The airplane has undeniable psycho-logical validity in the fact that man always wanted to fly. This has been the stuff of his fairy tales. And he has never stopped trying. But all his attempts failed until the Wright Brothers made it possible within the laws of nature and then nature said, "Okay, this is how I would have made it but I could never make it without first having been asked by man." In the same way, in bridging a river or a valley, the desire of man is to jump across in a single leap. The bridges of Robert Maillart, then, have that undeniable validity. It is the ingenuity of man to find ways to do things his way within the laws of nature and without having any prior examples to follow — to find that state where the desire to express (psychological validity) meets the instruments of expression (physical validity). This is where the pyramids began and the Greeks conceived the first column. This is the beginning of all human endeavors — "the threshold between Silence and Light."

The Place of Worship

1 First Unitarian Church
  Rochester, New York

2 Mikveh Israel
  Philadelphia, Pennsylvania

3 Convent for the Dominican Sisters
  Media, Pennsylvania

4 Saint Andrew's Priory
  Valyermo, California

5 Hurva Synagogue
  Jerusalem, Israel

The Place of Worship

Five projects presented on the same scale.

1 First Unitarian Church, Rochester, New York.
2 Mikveh Israel, Philadelphia, Pennsylvania.
3 Hurva Synagogue, Jerusalem, Israel.
4 Convent for the Dominican Sisters, Media, Pennsylvania.
5 Saint Andrew's Priory, Valyermo, California.

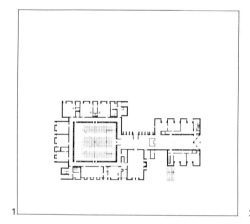

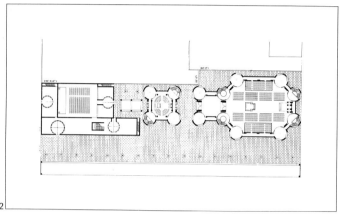

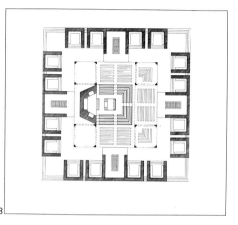

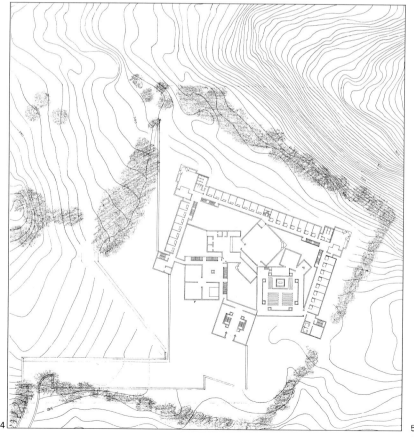

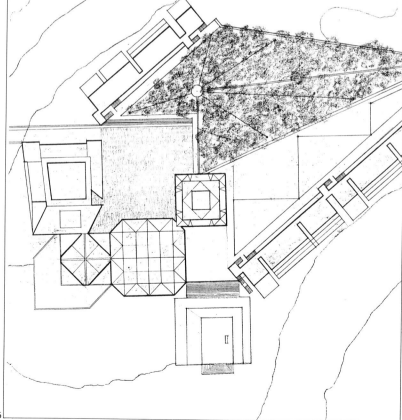

1 First Unitarian Church Rochester, New York

1959–1967

In the Unitarian Church, Kahn articulated his conception of the universal and circumstantial realities of form and design. Before arriving at the final solution, Kahn went through a series of schemes which, at each stage, came closer and closer to reconciling these dual realities, while the original theme of the sanctuary surrounded by the school remained.

The meeting hall is both stern and splendid; it is defined by cinder block wall and four hoods, which fill the room with light. The cinder block wall is made active by inte-

View of the entrance court looking west.

grating the supply and return air elements within it. The vertical slots in the wall are the return air elements.

Around this wall the classrooms, library, and kitchen each find shape appropriate to their functions. The exterior wall is modulated by light.

The materials are concrete, cinder block and brick.

An addition to the original building was completed in 1967.

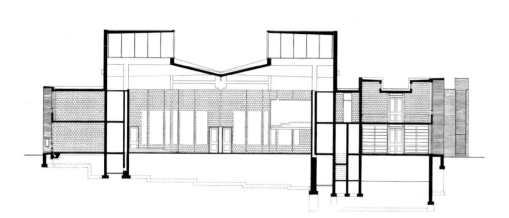

Section through the meeting-room and library looking north.

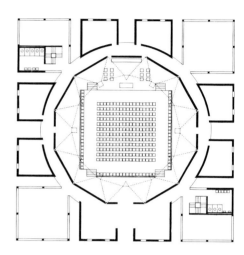

The first design. Diagrammatic transformation of form.

Ground-floor plan.

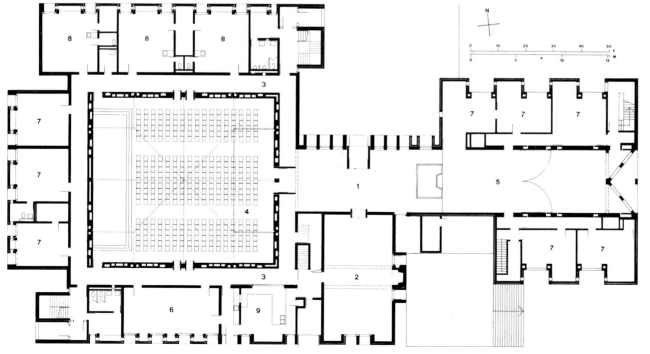

1 Entrance lobby
2 Library
3 Ambulatory
4 Meeting-room
5 Lounge
6 Workroom
7 Office
8 Class
9 Kitchen

An interior view of the meeting-room.

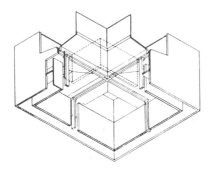

Isometric drawing of the meeting-room.

41

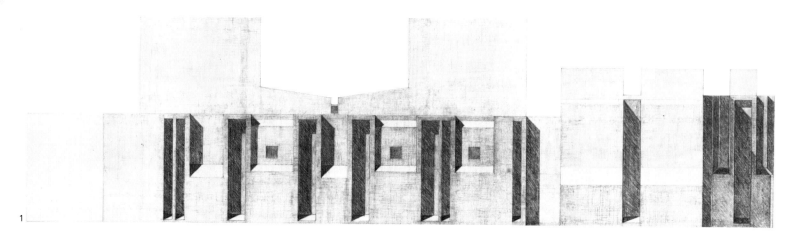

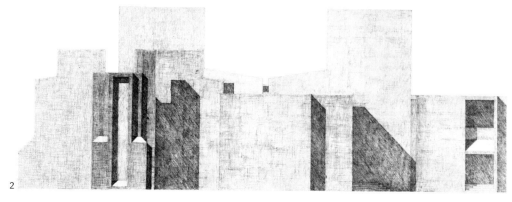

1 South elevation.
2 West elevation.
3 East elevation.
4 North elevation.

42

An interior view of the meeting-room.

2 Mikveh Israel
Philadelphia, Pennsylvania

Project 1961–1970

The synagogue is situated in the historic section of Philadelphia.

The plan is structured with a series of cylindrical "rooms" surrounding the sanctuary and chapel. Light penetrates through these cylinders and is diffused. Thus, light is given a volumetric form.

In the school building these volumes of light are reversed.

The primary materials are brick and concrete.

South view of model. The plan is drawn on the base of the model.

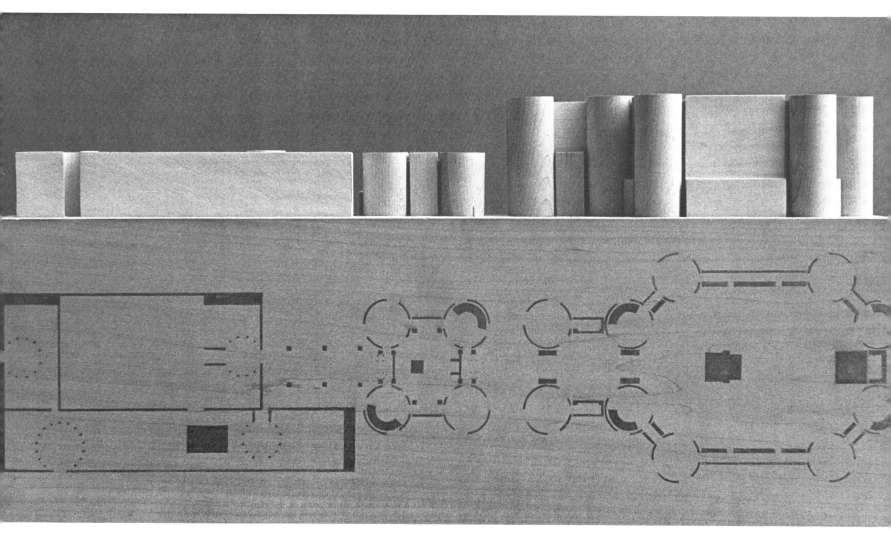

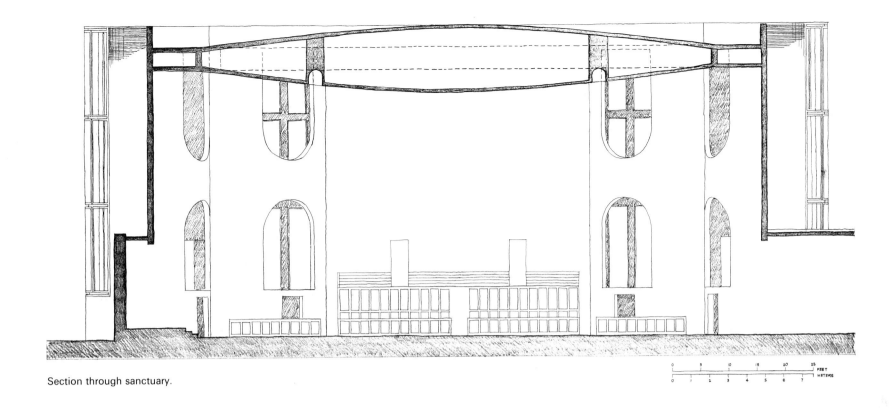

Section through sanctuary.

Plan.

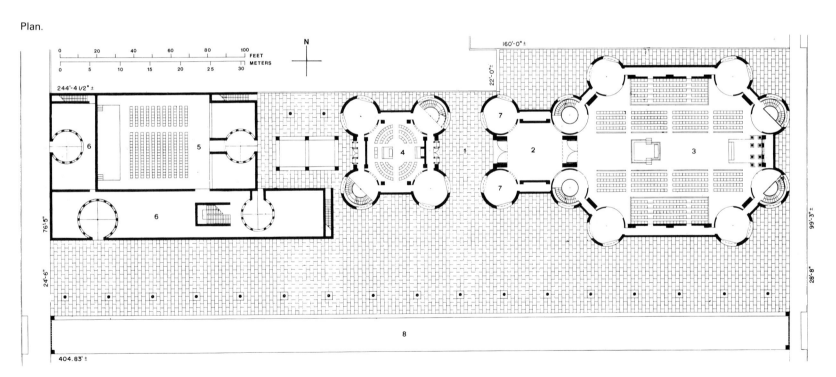

1 Entrance court
2 Entrance hall
2 Sanctuary
4 Chapel
5 Auditorium
6 School
7 Museum
8 Promenade

45

1

1   Entrance court.
2/3 View inside the sanctuary.

2

3

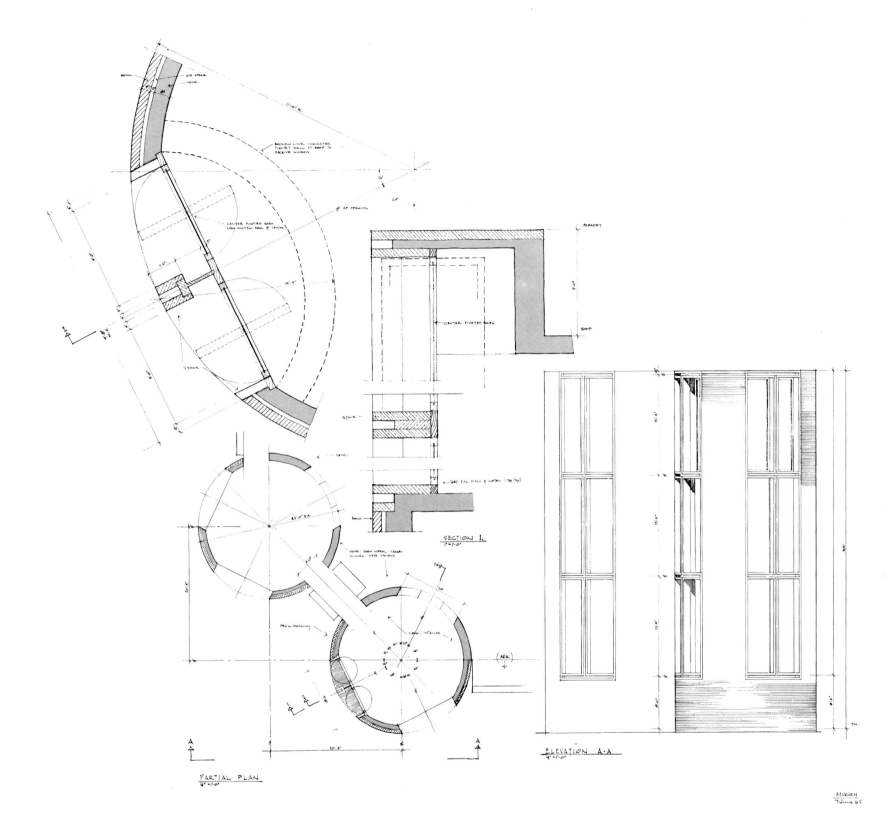

Working details for cylindrical light wells.

3 Convent for the Dominican Sisters Media, Pennsylvania

Project 1965–1968

Kahn felt from the beginning that the cell is a chapel for the individual. Thus the cells form an enclave defining the "village" of the community rooms.

The plan reflects the desire to connect without the use of elements such as corridors, which Kahn considers unnecessary.

The "tower" is the place of arrival. It contains meeting rooms for visitors, a library, chapter rooms and guest rooms.

The chapel is surrounded by an ambulatory, which serves also for procession to the refectory.

Study sketch showing early version of the entrance tower and sanctuary building.

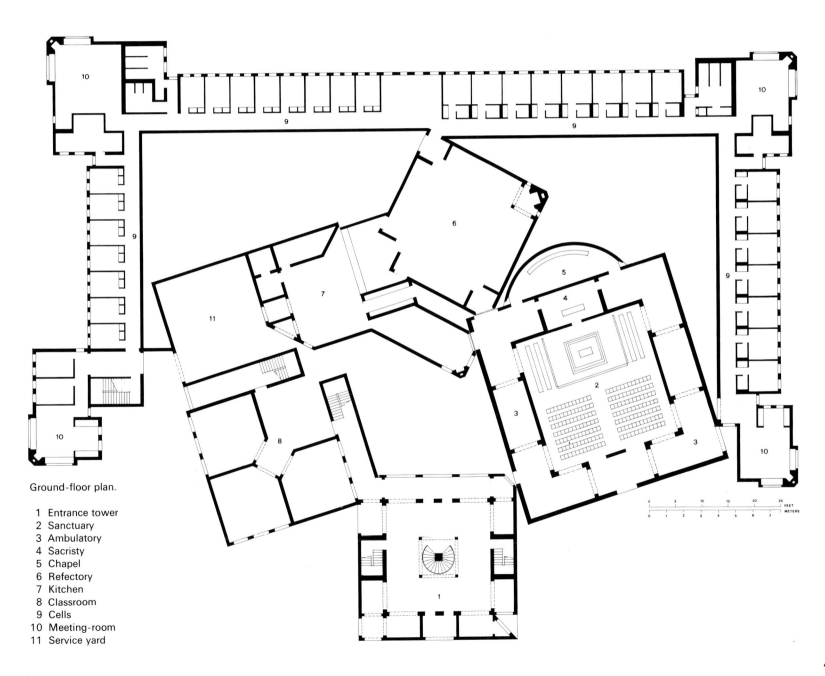

Ground-floor plan.

1 Entrance tower
2 Sanctuary
3 Ambulatory
4 Sacristy
5 Chapel
6 Refectory
7 Kitchen
8 Classroom
9 Cells
10 Meeting-room
11 Service yard

Elevation studies of an earlier scheme.

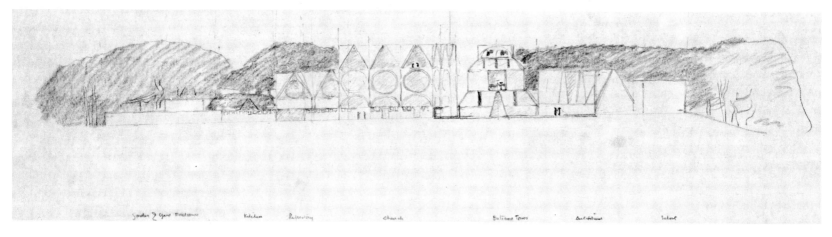

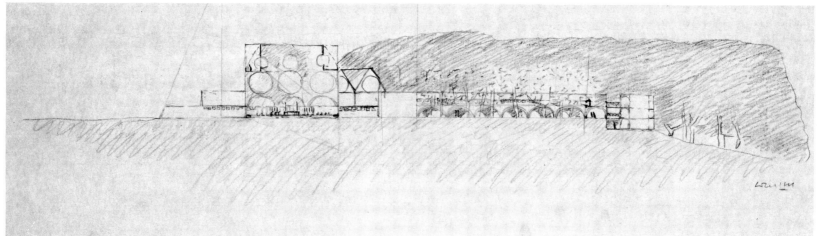

4 Saint Andrew's Priory Valyermo, California

Project 1966

The program is similar to the convent at Media, and both projects were done almost simultaneously.

The monastery sits on top of a hill and the plan recognizes the topography. The cells are placed on the side of the hill, and each cell has a terrace or a garden.

The landscape is barren and dry. The cloister garden is irrigated from the reservoir on top of the entrance tower.

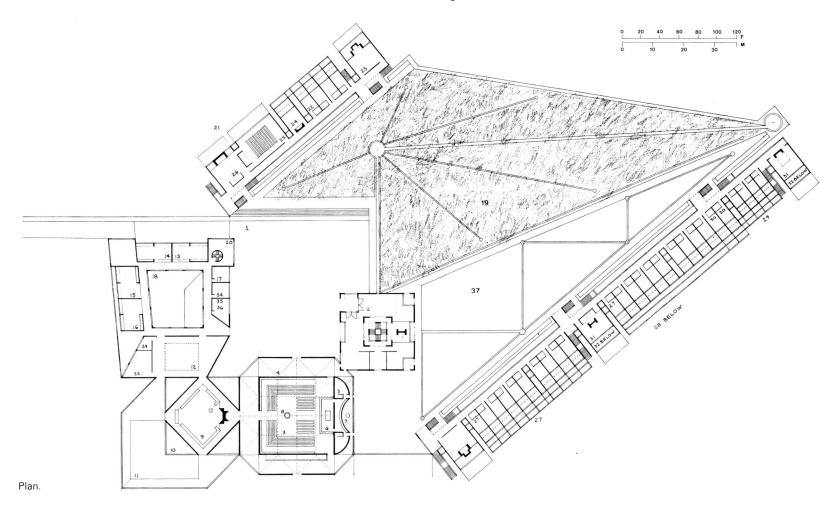

Plan.

1 Entrance court	11 Garden	26 Antechamber
2 Tower: Reception and administrative offices, library second floor, chapter-room third floor, reservoir and bell tower above, mechanical plant below	12 Kitchen and pantry	27 Monks cells: Fathers and professed monks cells (area: 12'4" × 22' including bathroom and closet)
	13 Small gallery	
	14 Ceramic shop	
	15 Metal-work shop	28 Cleric cells
	16 Mosaic-title shop	29 Novice cells
3 Church: Seating capacity: 300, Monks choir stalls: 72	17 Offices	30 Infirmary
	18 Work court	31 Common-rooms
4 Ambulatory	19 Cloister garden	32 Classrooms
5 Sacristy and vestry	20 Porch	33 Small dining-room for help
6 Altar	21 Guest wing	34 Barber shop
7 Shrine	22 Room with shower and basins	35 Tailor shop
8 Baptismal font	23 Reading-room	36 Laundry
9 Refectory	24 Visiting-rooms	37 Cloister court
10 Court	25 Auditorium	39 Kitchen office

Elevation study.

Section through cloister garden.

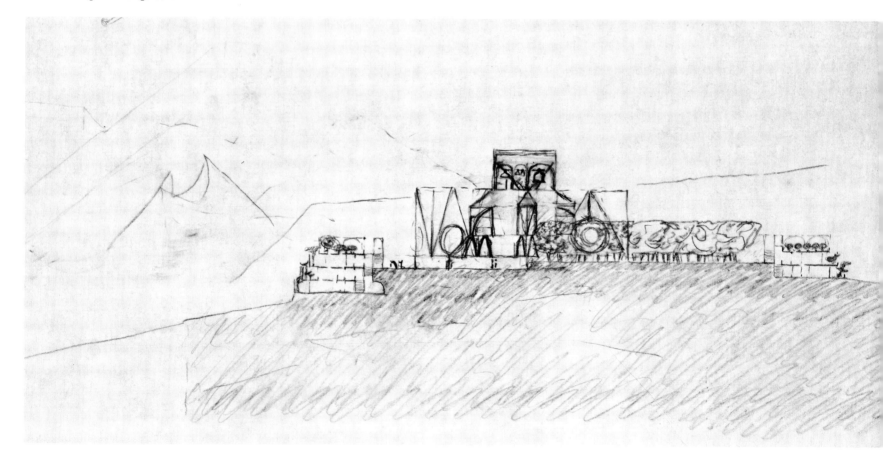

Site plan.

5 Hurva Synagogue
Jerusalem, Israel

Project 1968

The people of Jerusalem asked Louis Kahn to design a new synagogue on the site of the old one, which was destroyed during the war of independence. This new building is to be next to the ruins of the old synagogue.
The new synagogue is really two buildings, one wrapping around the other. The inner sanctuary, the place of worship, defined by four concrete umbrellas, is surrounded by a series of massive pyramid-shaped stone alcoves to be used for quiet reflection.
Kahn has also proposed linking the synagogue with the Wailing Wall by a series of places and institutions which will enhance the character of this historic city.

1 Model of the old city of Jerusalem. The proposed synagogue is on the left.
2 Upper-level plan.
3 Lower-level plan.
4 Sketch section and studies for roof structure.
5 Section through synagogue and part of the old city of Jerusalem.

1

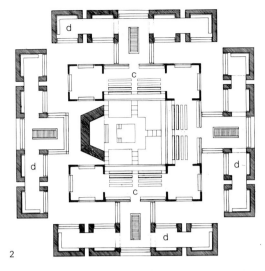

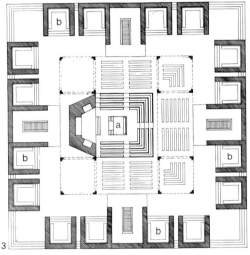

a Sanctuary
b Candle niches
c Upper gallery
d Upper part of candle niches

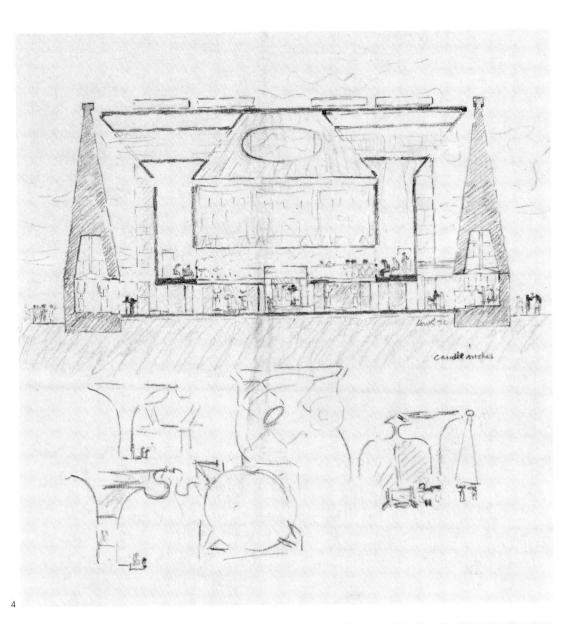

Model of synagogue.

View of interior.

The Sense of Place

Louis Kahn's perception of man is definitely linked to the concept of place; a concept to which he gave a particular sense. "Place" is a familiar word; it connotes an existence and, when reduced to human terms, a desire to be, to hold, and even, at times, to conquer. Place may assume the aspect of segregation or meeting, and always one of encounter with a natural site or an existing environment. The importance of place was particularly felt when it became obvious that the premises of the modern movement in architecture were bound to destroy the human reality of that sense in the assumptions of certain patterns of human behavior. Yet, in the existing architectural environment — the classic examples of ancient architecture all over the world — each one testified to a particular human condition, and the styles and language were telling of a characteristic aspiration: of celebration, intimacy, play, religion, etc. An extremely varied vocabulary of experience made possible the reduction of architecture to descriptive elements that gave an immediate understanding of the task assigned to the building.

This was true for both classic and gothic styles in architecture. Classic style proved itself so flexible that the gradual changes in the social structures, as well as the different places of the world where it was applied, did not make much difference to its basic formulation. Stylistic languages do not make a lot of difference in the evaluation of architecture; it is made, or a sense of it is related, only when aspects of human environment are touched. The shade and quietness of a porch in a Mexican farm house is a successful architecture in far greater measure than a technically well built or aesthetically up-to-date solution, since for the former, the commitment from the beginning was to make a place. A "sense of place" grew up, in time, to become a fundamental premise of contemporary architecture. It did not seem a preoccupation when the modern movement developed its themes. The reliance upon concepts, which codified modern movement through classicism and the beaux-arts, survived in many ways through modern experiences so that the basic understanding of place as a human environment was buried under the glorification of technology and functions.

The new architecture was still being considered under the parameters of abstract aesthetic expression, exactly like the old one, but the real issues were gradually coming to light. It took a while, as the built environment assumed incredible proportions, bound to self destruction and destruction of the natural environment. It took wars and an expanded materialism manifesting itself under different political systems and philosophies. It took the growing indifference of people to architecture, deriving from their reluctance to accept a highly rationalized view of expression by the architect. The debate in architecture assumed forms more and more tangential to the interests of the general public. It often became bound to political alternatives which made architecture an instrument of those interests and ideologies.

For Louis Kahn, place is not a physical entity that can retain a visual image completely. Only the confluence of a human program on the one hand and the natural character of a site on the other eventually produce a place. A place, thus, has an ideology, since it represents a human condition. All the subtle variations of such a condition are contained in it. A place is hardly a statement but, rather, the preparation for one through the careful play between the needs of man and of nature.

A place is indeed a presence, a more sophisticated situation than one generated by the precise, logical process of putting things together, the way an object is put together. A car or an airplane hardly makes a place; and a natural site, however impressive and capturing it may be, becomes a place only where man's presence is felt — an understanding, devoted presence realized within the very rules that nature has set for the agreement. Architecture may have started even before man erected four posts to make a roof. It started when he chose where to make it.

Thus, a sense of place was generated from the context of human issues, together with a natural site. Failure to understand this leads to a formal abstraction, which has little to do with architecture. Conversely, the attempt to resolve everything in natural terms leads to imitative efforts, which is a process that, although intended to be constructive, becomes destructive and proceeds to devaluate the very object to be exalted.

Louis Kahn's sense of place, on the contrary, stems from an archaic faith, which he consciously asserted in a world little concerned with faith. His places are for the life of society. His Salk Laboratory, the Richards Laboratory, the Exeter Library, the Museum at Fort Worth are places of unmistakable social character expressed as environments, wherein their spatial dimension corresponds exactly to the social dimension. Often his buildings are thought of as closed complexes, with solid walls outside which do not hint at the extreme articulation of their internal structure. This structural diversity corresponds to a dimensional diversity, which is meant to make a place for human accommodation inside and symbolic expression outside.

In exalting the idea of "institution," Louis Kahn, in effect, identifies "place" as being for the understanding of human actions, and in doing so he expresses the entire spectrum of human conditions which define it. From the Bath House of the Trenton Community Center to the penetrating spaces of Exeter — all contain the gradual transition from the dimension of the outside to the intimate recess of the room, from the public to the quasi-public to the private. All reproduce the gradual reduction of a context: the step from sound to silence, from the light of day to the measured light of a room, from the sharing of thoughts to reflections upon one's own thoughts. And this preoccupation remains the constant aspect of his architecture, an architecture which is, before the form of a plan or the shape of a roof, a search for a place which can make a person feel at home.

The Institutions

1 Yale University Art Gallery
New Haven, Connecticut

2 Salk Institute of Biological Studies
La Jolla, California

3 Indian Institute of Management
Ahmedabad, India

4 Philadelphia College of Art
Philadelphia, Pennsylvania

5 Library and Dining Hall,
Philip Exeter Academy
Exeter, New Hampshire

6 Kimbell Art Museum
Fort Worth, Texas

7 The Yale Center for British Art
and British Studies
New Haven, Connecticut

8 Wolfson Center for Mechanical
and Transportation Engineering,
University of Tel Aviv
Tel Aviv, Israel

The Institutions

1 Yale University Art Gallery, and the Yale Center for British Arts and British Studies, New Haven, Connecticut.
2 Salk Institute of Biological Studies, La Jolla, California.
3 Indian Institute of Management, Ahmedabad, India.
4 Philadelphia College of Art, Philadelphia, Pennsylvania.
5 Library and Dining Hall, Philip Exeter Academy, Exeter, New Hampshire.
6 Kimbell Art Museum, Fort Worth, Texas.
7 Wolfson Center for Mechanical and Transportation Engineering University of Tel Aviv, Israel.

Seven projects presented on the same scale.

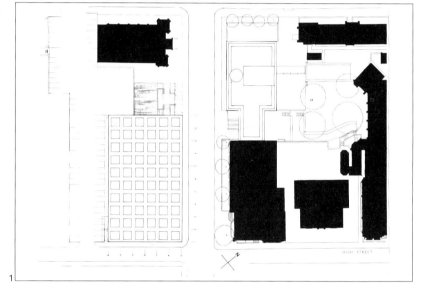

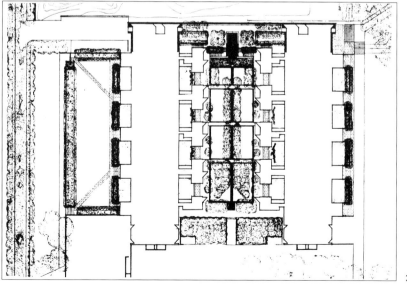

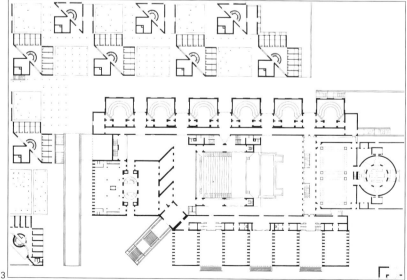

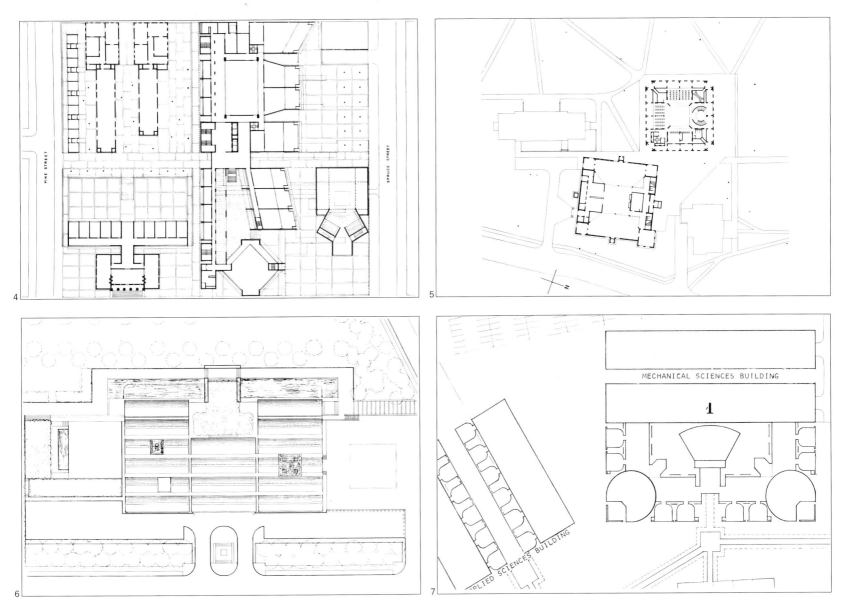

1 Yale University Art Gallery New Haven, Connecticut

1951–1953

Initially programmed to house the Department of Architecture in addition to the Art Gallery, the building is conceived as a simple loft space with a central core of elevators, stairways and utilities.

In order to provide the unimpeded flexibility needed for the different activities and different exhibitions, Kahn invented a new kind of reinforced concrete slab construction which integrated ceiling, floor and utility spaces in a single system of hollow tetrahedrons — thus eliminating the need for a hung ceiling. The division of this loft space is achieved by the use of a series of "pogo-panels."

The building is made of reinforced concrete, brick, and glass and steel curtain wall. All materials are left exposed.

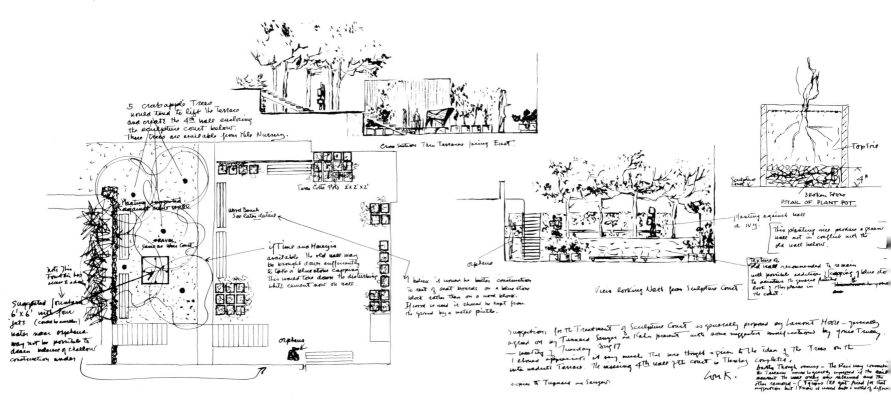

Sketches in a letter from Louis Kahn showing details of garden.

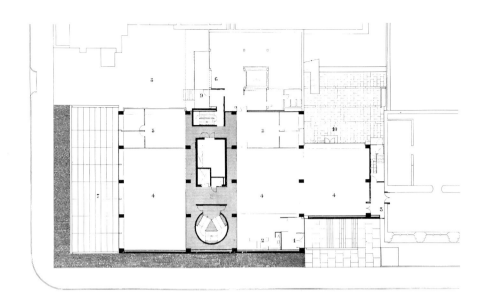

First-floor plan.

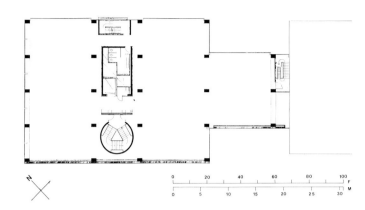

Fourth-floor plan.

1 Entrance
2 Reception
3 Vestibule
4 Gallery
5 Office
6 Storage
7 Court
8 Service yard
9 Loading dock
10 Garden (lower level)

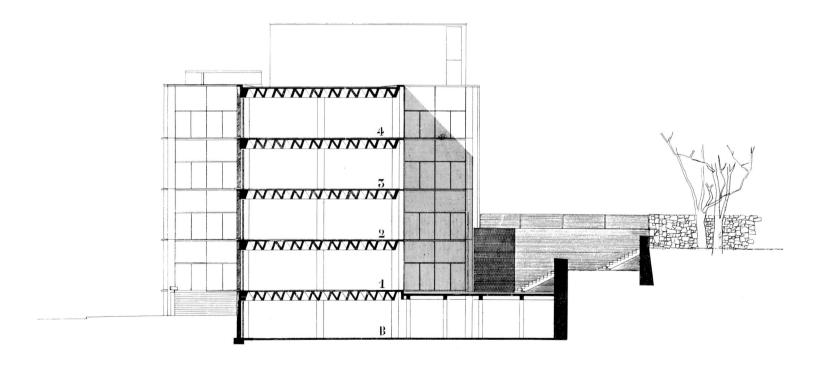

Cross section through the gallery and garden.

1 View looking north-east.
2 View from the lower-level garden.
3 Exhibition gallery.

3

2 Salk Institute of Biological Studies La Jolla, California

1959–1965
Structural Engineer: August Komendant

Dr. Salk, who had made an exhaustive survey of laboratory buildings before he saw the one at the University of Pennsylvania, wanted a place not only for biological research but also a place where he could "invite a man like Picasso."
The meeting hall and the residence quarters are not yet built.

Model photo.

Site plan.

1 Laboratory building
2 Meeting house
3 Staff housing

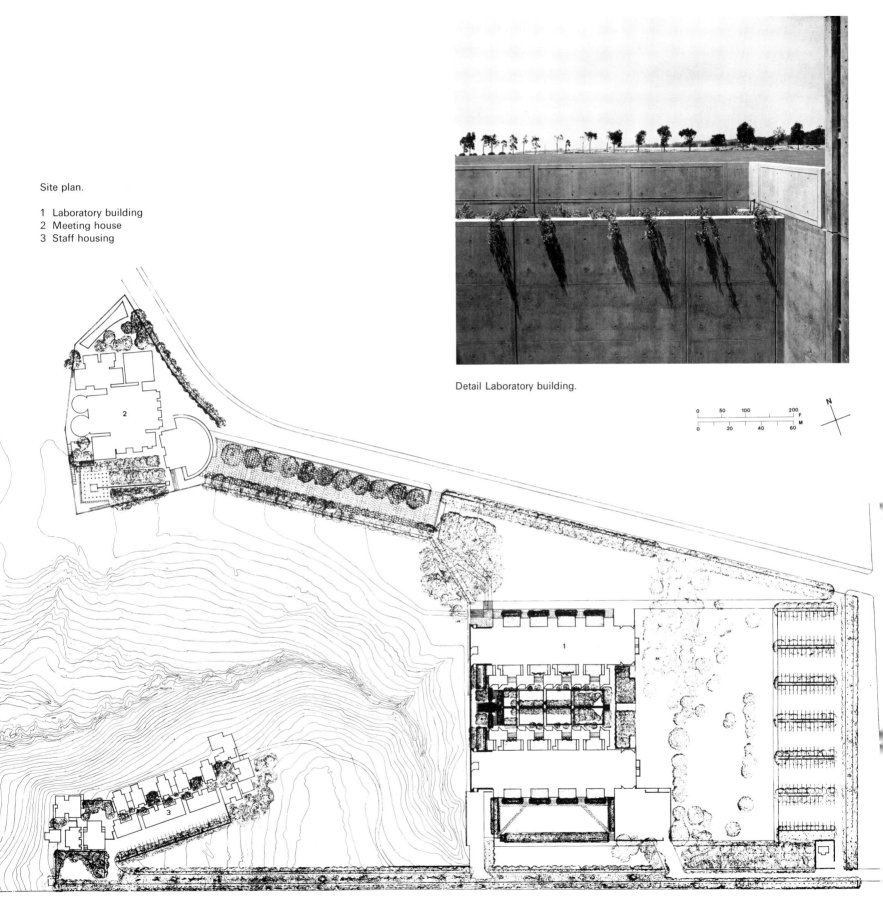

Detail Laboratory building.

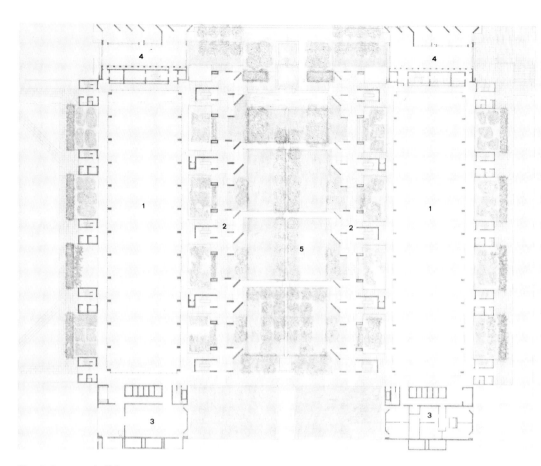

Plan Laboratory building.

The laboratories are in clear loft spaces made possible by story-high vierendeel trusses, which also provide integral "rooms" for the utilities. The small study areas are separated from the work spaces and are placed on alternate floors on the level of the utilities.

1 Laboratory
2 Loggia (study room above)
3 Office
4 Library
5 Garden Court

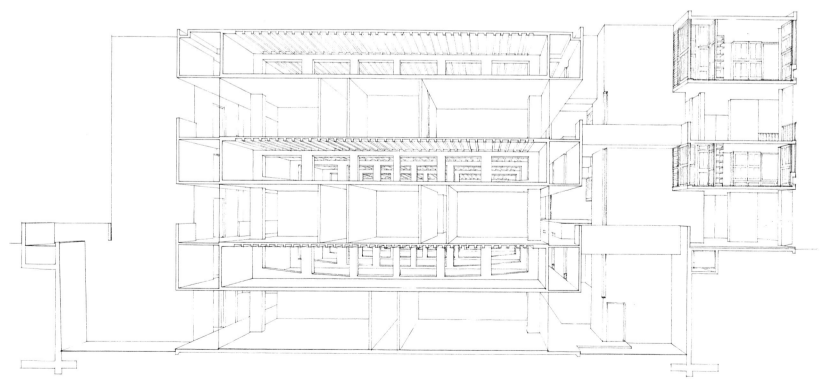

Section through laboratory wing.

Model photo of an earlier scheme.

An earlier solution to integration of structure and utilities.

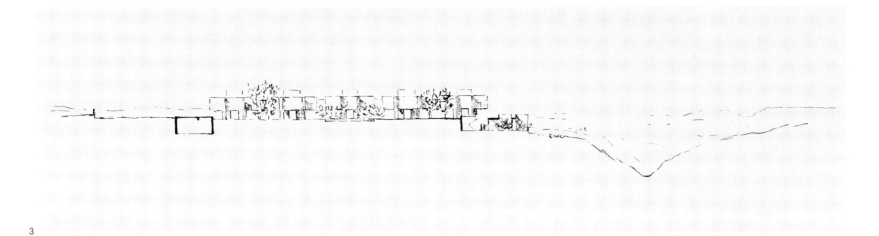

3

1 Model photo, meeting house.
2 Model photo. Front administration, rear laboratories (early version).
3 Section through staff housing.

Study sketches, meeting house.

The separation of the study rooms from laboratories is further emphasized by the diagonal of stair leading up to the study rooms.

◁ View from the "loggia" floor. The small study areas are situated above and below (see also page 74).

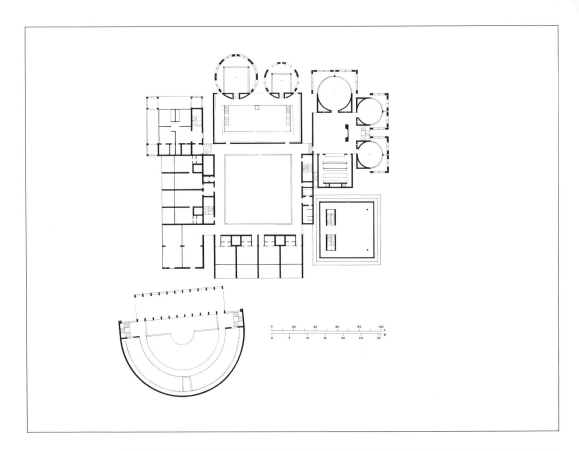

Second-floor plan.

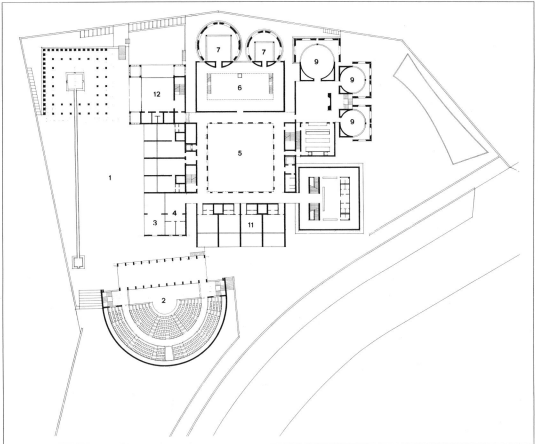

First-floor plan, Meeting house.

1 Garden
2 Auditorium
3 Entrance porch
4 Entrance
5 Banquet hall
6 Library
7 Reading-room
8 Kitchen
9 Dining
10 Gymnasium
11 Guest
12 Directors quarters

3 Indian Institute of Management Ahmedabad, India

1963   Under construction

In a city of intense cultural, commercial, and political vitality, Kahn's new complex is an addition to an already fine collection of magnificent architecture, both old and new.

The peculiar social and environmental demands of the location have directed both the organization of activities and the formal language. The three elements — the school, the dormitories, and the teachers' residences — are grouped to take advantage of the available winds, to provide as much uninterrupted breeze through the buildings as possible. At the same time, the penetration of hot sun and glaring light is minimized by incorporating covered verandas, light wells, and court yards as integral elements of the architectural vocabulary.

The site plan suggests the relationship between the school, the dormitories, and the teachers' residences. The school and the dormitories are expressed as a unit, like a monastery; their unity is emphasized by placing a lake between the dormitories and the residences.

Brick is the material most readily available in India. The formal language of the entire complex is determined by an attempt to fully exploit brick as a structural material.

Site model of the entire complex.

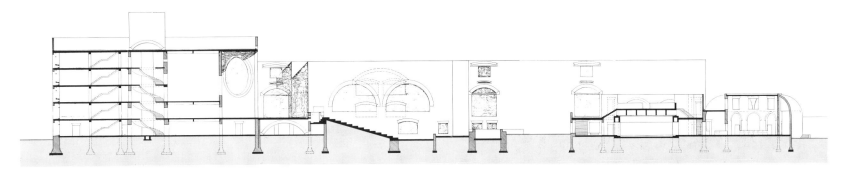

Longitudinal section through school building.

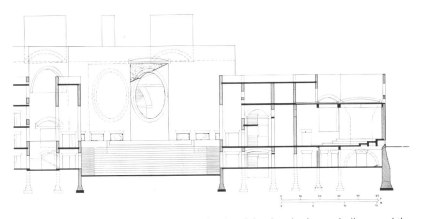

Cross section through school. Both the school and the dormitories are built around the idea of meeting. The school is organized around a court yard and an amphitheater, while in the dormitories, the usual corridor gives way to deep triangular ''porches'' where meeting is possible.

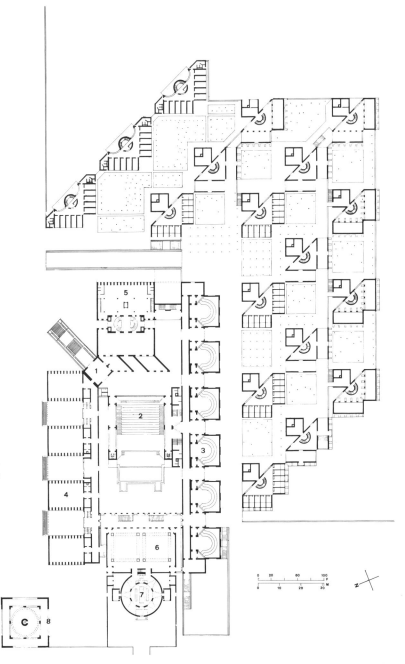

Plan School building.

1 Entrance
2 Amphitheater
3 Classroom
4 Offices
5 Library
6 Dining
7 Kitchen
8 Water tower

Details of composite construction of brick and concrete — School building.

Dormitory.

1 Hall
2 Kitchen
3 Dining
4 Upper part of dining
5 Rooms
6 Toilets

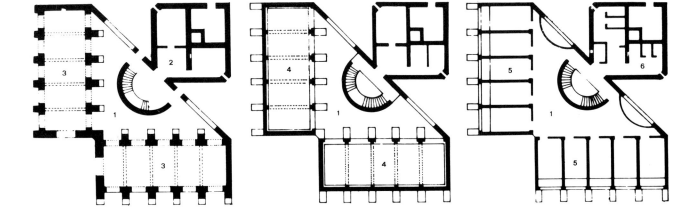

Ground-floor plan.

Second-floor plan.

Typical upper floor.

Detail of the curved masonry wall.

Lakeside view of dormitories.

Exterior detail at entrance of dormitory.

1/2 Elevation studies of faculty housing.
3 Section study.
4 Ground floor.
5 Upper floor.
6 South-west view.
7 Rear view of a typical row of housing units.

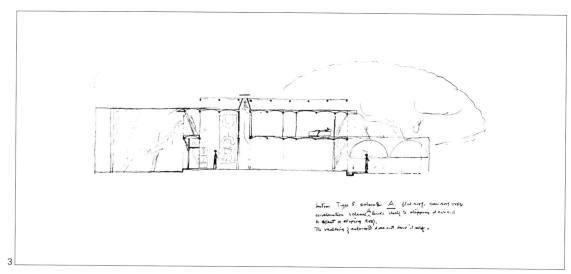

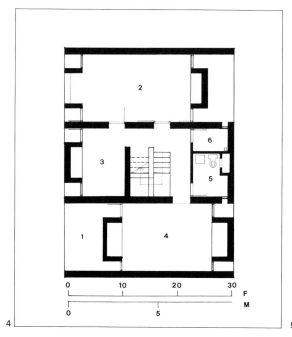

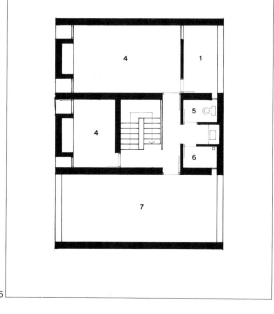

1 Porch
2 Living-room
3 Kitchen
4 Bedroom
5 Toilet
6 Bath
7 Terrace

6

7

The main entrance stair of school building under construction.

View of dormitories. In the foreground is the classroom wing under construction.

4 Philadelphia College of Art
Philadelphia, Pennsylvania

Project 1964–1967

The project is located in the busy downtown section of Philadelphia on the main thoroughfare. The awareness of this intensely urban location is expressed not only in the way the building participates in the making of the city, but also in the way it makes one aware of the possibilities of the city. The formal organization of the building, both in its massiveness and in its arrangement of parts, reflects the intensity of the urban environment outside.

The plan is structured around two interior courts, which are open to the sky. Studios and workshops are on the side facing north, while classrooms, offices, and locker areas are located on the southern side of the courtyards. A large exhibition hall with library and reading room above is at the end facing Broad Street.

The building was designed to accommodate the expansion of an existing institution which already possesses some fine buildings.

Study sketch. Broad-Street elevation.

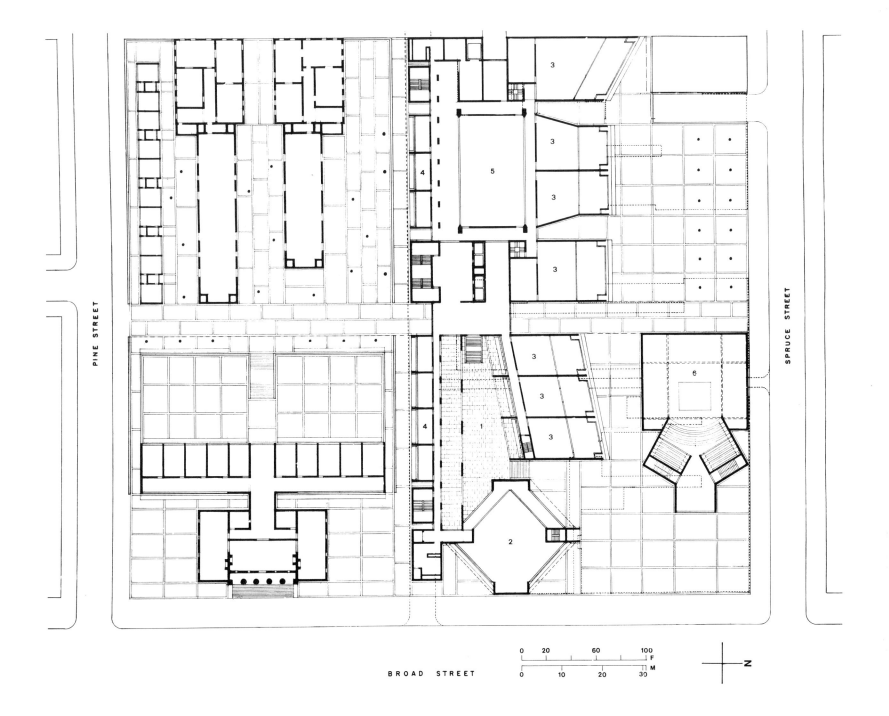

PINE STREET

SPRUCE STREET

BROAD STREET

0   20   60   100
|————|————|————|————|————| F
0   10   20   30 M

N

Entrance-floor plan.

1 Entrance hall
2 Exhibition hall
3 Studios
4 Offices
5 Open court
6 Auditorium

87

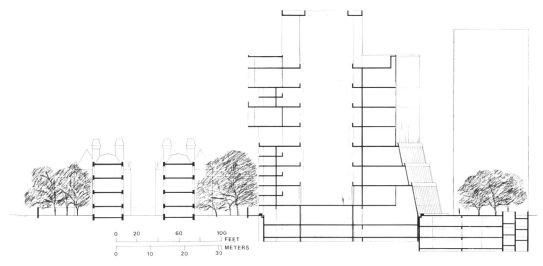

Cross-section through open court.

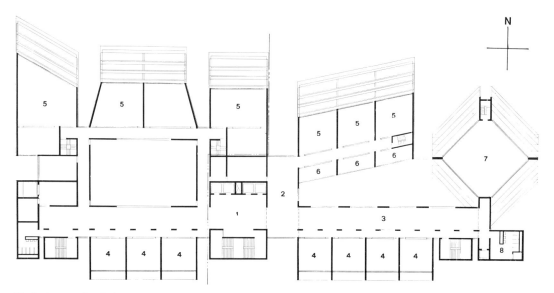

Typical upper-level plan.

1 Elevator lobby
2 Lobby
3 Gallery
4 Classrooms
5 Studios
6 Small studios or storage
7 Upper library reading-room
8 Toilets

The Broad Street view. The existing school is on the left.

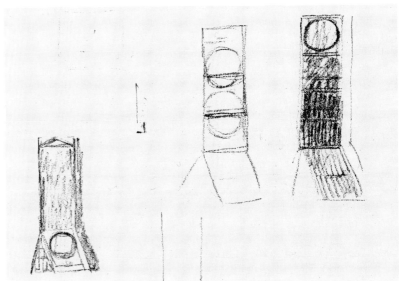

Study sketches for the Library Tower.

5 Library and Dining Hall, Philip Exeter Academy Exeter, New Hampshire

1967–1972

This new building, situated in a fine New England rural setting, is a composite of two distinct elements of a library: the storage of books — with their great mass, weight, and need to be kept away from light — and a person being alone with a book where the light is.

The conventional large "reading hall" is rejected in recognition of the fact that reading is a private activity. Instead, the periphery of the building consists of a series of small reading areas or carrels. This outer "doughnut," which is made of brick masonry construction, surrounds the inner "doughnut" of concrete, where books are stored away from strong light. The idea of a library as a "sanctuary of books and ideas" is symbolized by the great entrance hall in the center.

All the elements are clearly articulated and are uncompromising in their construction.

The dining hall consists of two large dining rooms and four smaller areas, all served by a central service area in the middle. Light enters from large skylights around the center. The smaller dining rooms on the corners are filled with light from generous windows.

The major materials for both the library and the dining hall are brick and concrete with wood for doors and windows. The roof of the dining hall is made of precast concrete planks. All materials are left exposed.

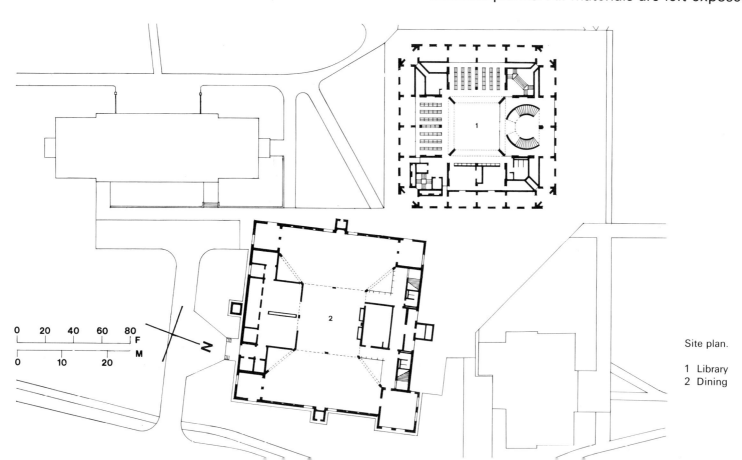

Site plan.

1 Library
2 Dining

Library — South-west façade.

1 Central hall
2 Reference and periodicals
3 Books
4 Carrels
5 Fireplace
6 Toilets

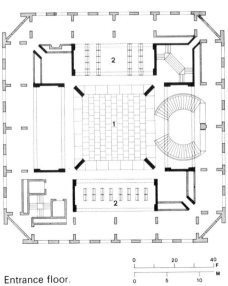

Entrance floor.

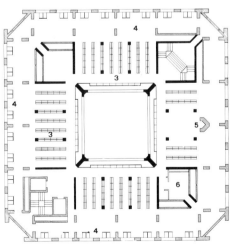

Third floor.

The reading area on the periphery.

The central hall.

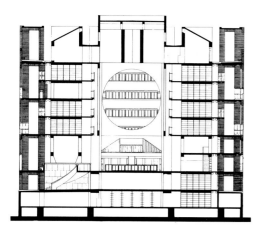

Sketch of library. The low building on the left is the dining hall.

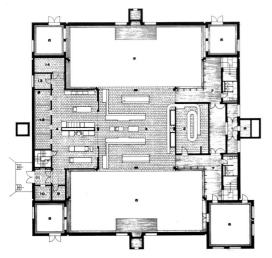

Ground floor.

1 Entrance
2 Dish washing
3 Serving
4 Food preparation
5 Dining
6 Private dining
7 Books and coats
8 Storage
9 Can wash
10 Garbage
11 Loading
12 Freezers
13 Office
14 Dry storage

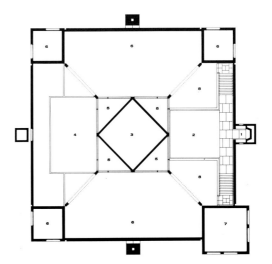

Mezzanine.

1 Fireplace
2 Lounge
3 Cooking tower enclosure
4 Kitchen below
5 Light well
6 Dining below
7 Private dining below
8 Open to below

6 Kimbell Art Museum
Fort Worth, Texas

1967–1972

The museum sits in a garden, with ample land around it. This prompted the decision that it should be a low building, which can borrow light from the roof.

The collection consists of relatively small objects of the 19th century and earlier art. Because they were created in natural light, Kahn felt that they should be viewed in natural light.

Kahn conceived two kinds of light: a "silver light" which comes from the sky and a "green light" which comes through the plants in the three courts, which intercept the cycloids.

The skylights are made with perforated aluminum elements which reflect the light back to the concave surface of the cycloids. The shape of both the cycloids and the aluminum elements is calculated for an even distribution of light.

Interior view of Gallery. The door on the right leads to one of the three courts.

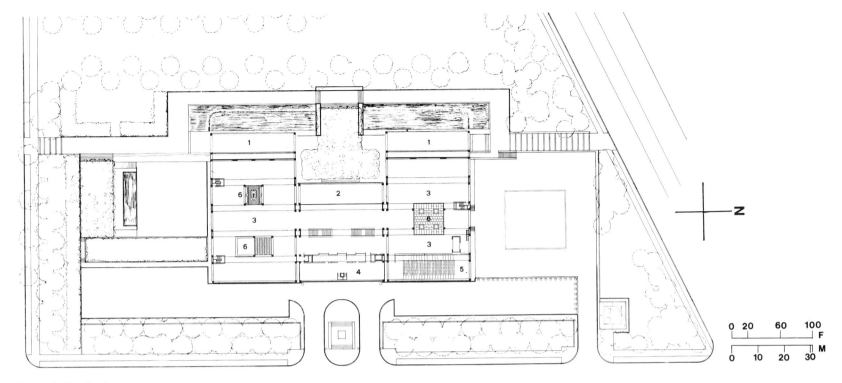

Plan – Gallery level.

1 Porch
2 Entrance
3 Gallery
4 Book sale
5 Auditorium
6 Open court

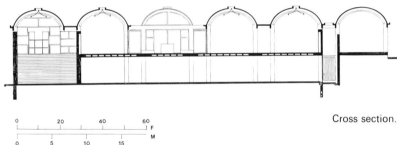

Cross section.

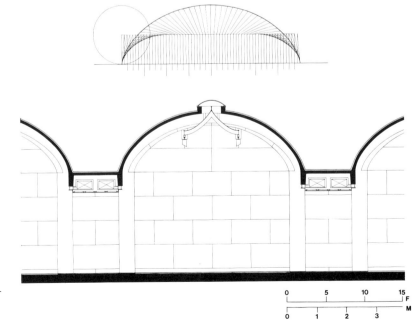

The plan is made of repeatable units – "rooms" – which have an existence independent of the plan form. These are 20 feet wide with a variable length.
They are placed alternately between low "servant" spaces.

◁ Two study sketches.

Interior view of Gallery.

7 The Yale Center for British Art and British Studies New Haven, Connecticut

1969   Under construction

The building is designed to house paintings, prints and books.

The structure is made of concrete frame with in-fill panels. The non-bearing nature of the in-fill panels is expressed by the materials from which they are made — stainless steel on the exterior and white oak on the interior.

The entire roof is made of specially designed skylights, which also contain supply air elements. Other utilities are housed in the hollow slab.

View from lower court. Shops are located on the periphery of the court, as well as entrance to the auditorium.

◁ View of museum from the road.

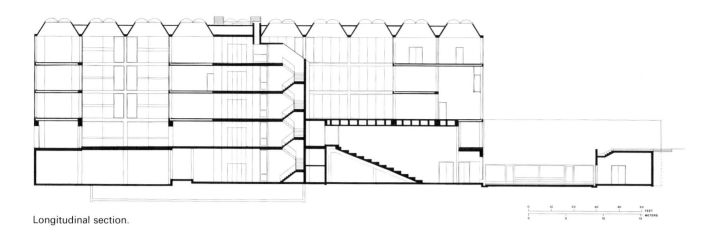

Longitudinal section.

Fourth-floor plan.

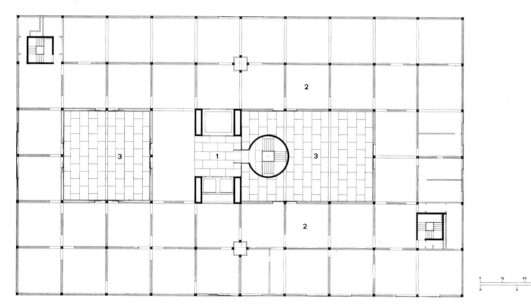

1 Lobby
2 Gallery
3 Light Court

Street-level plan.

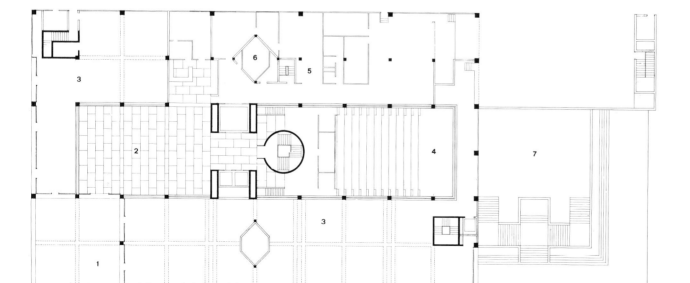

1 Entrance porch
2 Court
3 Shops
4 Auditorium
5 Service
6 Air duct
7 Lower court and shops

View from Chapel Street, looking north-west.

South façade. The Yale Art Gallery can be seen in the left background.

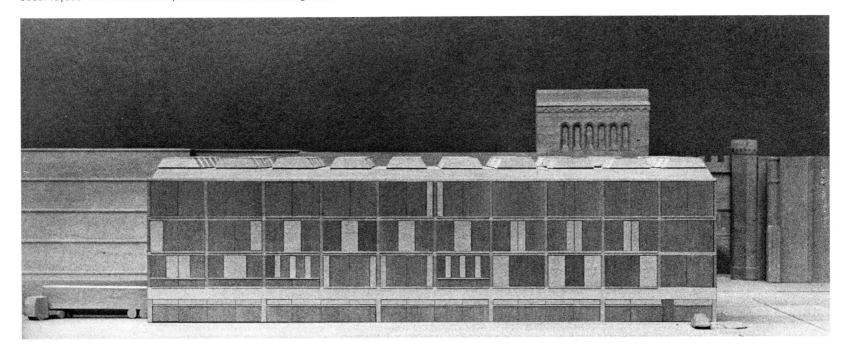

View of the interior light court from third floor.

View of the interior light court from fourth floor.

8 Wolfson Center for Mechanical and Transportation Engineering, University of Tel Aviv
Tel Aviv, Israel

1968   Under construction

The Center is a part of a larger plan which consolidated different engineering departments. A sunken, shaded path connects the engineering campus with the rest of the university. The library is conceived as a gateway to the engineering campus.

Concrete is the primary building material, as in most buildings in Israel.

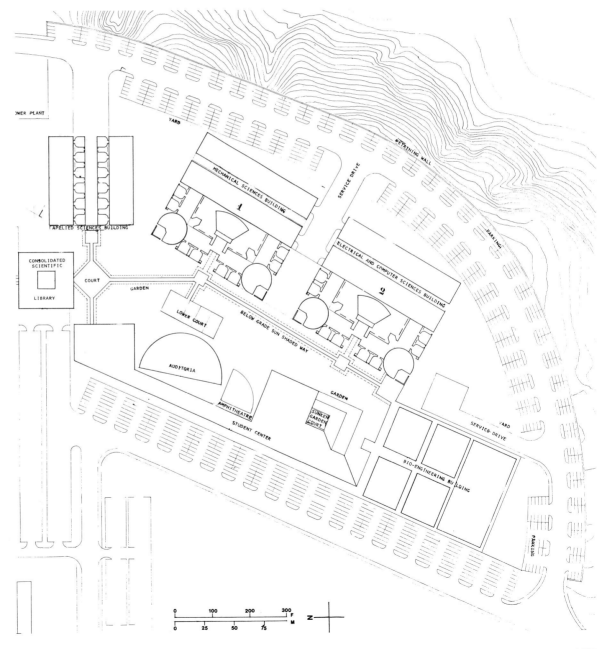

Site plan of the entire engineering campus.

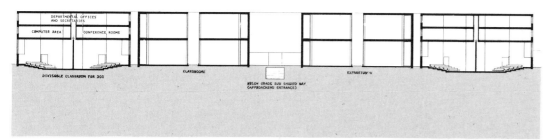

Section C-C.

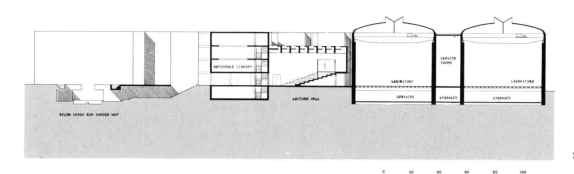

Section A-A.

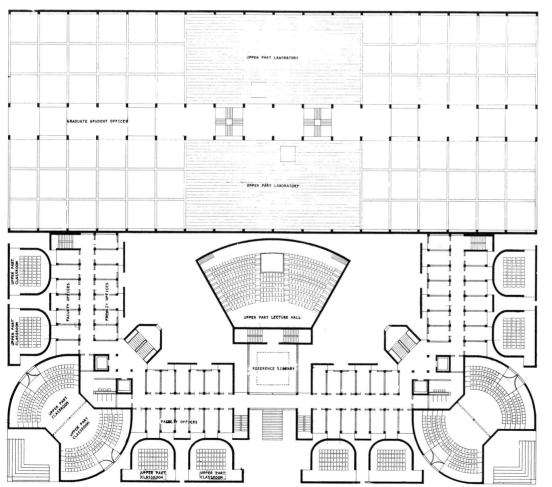

Second-floor plan.

The elevation towards the garden.

The Institutions of Man

The America of Louis Kahn is not the same as that of Thomas Jefferson, or of Frank Lloyd Wright, or of Mies or Gropius. It is not the America defined by the optimism of a new beginning or the hopes of the New Deal. It is a country involved in a revolution of human and social values much deeper than it appears. It is a country where the contradictions of today's knowledge are developing into new human choices which transform the places of our accommodations. And these choices are directed less toward the exploits of technological successes and more and more for the real warmth of human contact. These are the signs of new beginnings, new possibilities — a contradictory world where the contradictions of attempting to write poetry without words give the true measure of our situation, and where a coherent architectural dimension is indeed obtainable.

That is why Kahn can avoid being a polemecist. He can look at the past as at a personal experience and reach, at times, for the same architectural conclusion as one dedicated to the present. This discovery is associated with the re-discovery of things that man seems always to look for — the things that have accompanied the human struggle from the primordials and have formed the main points for a structural relationship.

We owe to Kahn a re-definition of the term "institution." If the contradictions of the time point toward the tentative nature of things, the institution is an expression of the common belief of a people. An idea rather than an entity, it expresses those aspects of human life upon which an agreement has been felt — a principle or an order which, by the virtue of having this power to gener-

ate the consent of fellow humans, stems from the commonalities in human nature. What inspired the beginning of institutions is of tremendous value, for it is not the actual circumstances of their beginning that matter — they tell only us of the needs of the time which are temporal. An eternal agreement is a sign of the inevitable which transcends time. Unless a building strives to serve this eternal agreement, and unless its spatial elements have this inevitability about them, its architecture will remain only corrective. But the purpose of architecture does not stop at problem-solving; it involves translating into a spatial language the inevitable aspects of human institutions.

"Existence will" is only another way of saying inevitable. Nothing which has any lasting value comes into being by the hands of man unless its inevitability is felt by man. Thus, when Kahn says that something has an "existence will," or that a rose wants to be a rose and a large opening in a brick wall wants an arch, he is only stating the simple fact that there is something inevitable about all these.

This belief in "institution," in the inevitability of things, is in intimate rapport with the discipline of architecture — a discipline which neither ignores nor worships the utilitarian values but, at the same time, seeks to express the common denominators in human phenomena that are not affected by the current notions of efficiency and rational organization. This sense of discipline is often rejected by the impatience of our time, an impatience which is also a sign of a dilemma of commitment among architects. On the one hand we are pulled by the need to be universally valid, to be objective beyond controversy, and to measure our work by only the most rational criteria. This has often led to indifference toward specific human values, a situation which makes architecture more and more dependent on rationally organized technological and administrative systems. On the other hand, this very worship of reason has resulted in a sense of not belonging, of a lack of belief in any specific architectural or cultural values. This, in turn, leads from architecture to circumstantial solutions. It is Kahn's uncompromising search for the fundamental and inevitable elements in architecture which puts him in possession of a method of judgment that looks beyond the urgency of the moment, not with passive indifference to it, but in search of that common beginning which will help make critical distinctions between the universal and the particular. This method of judgment leads to actions that have human validity beyond social, ethnic, or racial considerations. It does not require an encyclopedic knowledge, only an ability to comprehend that the concept of truth is not really different from the concept of validity as applied to human endeavors. "Institution," like city, like architecture, is the place and the moment for the consolidation of these endeavors.

There are three constants in Kahn's investigation of the institutions of man: 1) the School, 2) the Street, and 3) the Village Green. The "School" epitomizes all the places that are dedicated to man's desire to learn — not so much the acquisition of practical knowledge as a comprehension of the nature of one's own being, of one's relationships to another, and the relationship between man and nature. Such a consciousness of the most fundamental inspirations of man allows Kahn to translate and transform a programmatic need of education into a spatial environment of learning. The "Street" stands for all the places of meeting and availabilities. "Street" is where a person becomes aware of what opportunities and instruments are available to him to express the nature of his being. If we think of a city as an environment of infinite availabilities, or — as Kahn puts it — "where a boy growing up can find out what he wants to be when he grows up," the "Street" becomes the very essence of the city. All places of man where the singularity of one individual comes in contact with that of another belong to the "Street," the institution of meeting. Through meeting and through the exchange of ideas and talents, one is introduced to new opportunities, new ways of doing things.

In the "Village Green," Kahn consolidates all those activities of man whereby the desires of one man and that of others find a resolution as a common direction of a people; as a place of mind, it is a "forum," a place of representation and consideration of validities.

Thus, when Kahn refers to "School" or "Street" or "Village Green" as the fundamental institutions, he is referring to all the places that have an undeniable and inevitable affinity with man's desire to learn, to meet to express, and for well-being and freedom. There is a sense here of the fundamental activities of man. Here Kahn is working within the realization of the individual — his homecoming, his departures, his scale to the place and to nature — a man neither smarter than his predecessors nor more vile, a man capable of translating his experience of life into essential form. Few architects have placed more attention on the subtle transition of human activities — from work to relaxation to play to comfort — reaching for simple dignity in the acts of life. It is such attention to "the present" that becomes dramatically operative in the architecture of Louis Kahn as new necessities are revealed and what is ephemeral becomes distinguishable from what is permanent. This is like saying that cities are reborn on a more just human rapport.

If there can be an "architecture of society," institutions would provide its structure. For it is the strength inherent in the institutions that will determine whether a society is capable of meeting the challenge of its own momentum. In America, if the decade of the nineteen sixties failed to live up to the hopes and aspirations of the New Deal and the New Frontiers, it certainly brought to the fore the vulnerability and the frailty of American institutions — institutions which were founded on efficiency and reason, which are values of an industrial civilization. However, rationality — which holds reason to be the supreme human value as well as goal — has limits in engineering social change, for it excludes those aspects of human life which cannot be subjected to the analytical methods of reason.

Seen within such a framework, Kahn's sense of institution manifests his vision of a society. The institution he considers fundamental offers a plan of a society which is totally consistent with his sense of man. Such a society is built upon the most fundamental and timeless aspects of human existence. It is on such ground that the principles proposed by Louis Kahn may be developed and where architecture may once again find its formative constant, where it may establish the locus of human things, both on an intimate and public level.

The street is a room by agreement: a community room, the walls of which belong to the donors, dedicated to the city for common use. Its ceiling is the sky. From the street must have come the meeting house, also a place by agreement.

The School

"When I speak about the emergence of new institutions, I am also thinking of the review of present institutions. I feel the institutions of man come from the inspirations of man. The inspiration to learn stems from the way we were made. Everything that nature makes it records in what it makes, how it was made. In the rock is the record of the rock. In man is the record of man. And through our gift of consciousness in, I would believe, the hierarchy of consciousness, in which I believe even the rose has consciousness of its kind, or every living things has, there is this affinity for the great history of how we were made, and some are endowed with the ability to reconstruct the entire universe just by knowing a blade of grass. The inspiration to learn is the source of all institutions of learning – they inspire the institutions of learning.

"I think of 'School' as an environment of spaces where it is good to learn. Schools began with a man under a tree who did not know he was a teacher discussing his realization with a few who did not know they were students. The students reflected on what was exchanged and how good it was to be in the presence of this man. They aspired that their sons also listen to such a man. Soon spaces were erected and the first schools became. The establishment of School was inevitable because it was part of the desires of man.

"The realization of what particularizes the domain of spaces good for School would lead an institution of learning to challenge the architect to awareness of what School 'wants to be' which is the same as saying what is the form, School."

The Street

"If you think of the street as a meeting place, if you think of a street as being really a community inn that just doesn't have a roof. And if you think of a meeting hall, it is just a street with a roof on it. If you think of it in terms of meeting. And the walls of this meeting place called the community room, the Street, are just the fronts of the houses, and the streets were dedicated by the houses to the city for their use. Today those streets are disinterested movements not at all belonging to the houses that front them. So you have no streets. You have roads, but you have no streets. To bring back the streets: to make redefined movement and place movement in an order of movement where the Street takes its rightful position as belonging to the community of communication. I think you can straighten out your plans very easily. I would start with that, very simply. You just are really defining the rightful demand of houses to bring their streets back. I think the character of the streets would change enormously if that were done."

The Village Green

"In the University there should be desire, in the marketplace there's need, and the place between, the forum, should be the place where need and desire are both considered.

"I think that it comes to being in my mind thinking about the Centennial, and the kind of buildings the [Centennial] should have... it is just that kind of place. The

[Centennial], you see, is the place which is between the marketplace and between the pure theoretical presentations of the University.

"A Man's work may be making money, his work may be a blacksmith, his work may be something else, a preacher, but his representation is somehow, in the 'Village Green,' tempered the moment he is in the Village Green with the desires of others, realizing that if he only wanted something himself, he would not get it. So he needs the place where what he wants is also what other people want, which allows him to have what he wants, and allows others also to have. So in the place of representation, where representation really is felt for its particular directions in entrusting, let's say, the governing of a nation which has to do with the release of funds and the release of law for the establishing of the institutions, you have the sense that you're being protected, that the government is that kind of thing, and that representation is understood. I'm very concerned about this, with representation, because I feel as though the 'Village Green' has been lost to us, and during the traffic of things and thinking always of the new institutions of man. I cannot but think of a new place of representation, and it constantly goes to a new kind of green, Village Green, which is, after all, not a village green but is the place where the plan, you might say the horse-sense of the day, is. Desire and need is horse-sense."

The Place of Well-Being

1 Trenton Jewish Community
Center
Trenton, New Jersey

Theater of Performing Arts
Fort Wayne, Indiana

2 Fort Wayne Fine Arts Center
Fort Wayne, Indiana

3 "Interama," Inter-American
Community
Florida

4 "Banglanagar," Capital Complex
of Bangladesh
Dacca, Bangladesh

5 Capital Complex of Western
Pakistan
Islamabad, Pakistan

6 Memorial to Six Million Jews
New York City

7 Congress Hall
Venice, Italy

8 Inner Harbor Project
Baltimore, Maryland

9 Family Planning Center
Kathmandu, Nepal

10 Pocono Art Center
Pennsylvania

11 Franklin Delano Roosevelt
Memorial
Roosevelt Island, New York

The Place of Well-Being

Ten projects presented on the same scale.

1 Trenton Jewish Community Center, Trenton, New Jersey.
2 Fort Wayne Fine Arts Center, Fort Wayne, Indiana.
3 "Interama," Inter-American Community, Florida.
4 "Banglanagar," Capital Complex of Bangladesh, Dacca, Bangladesh.
5 Capital Complex of Western Pakistan, Islamabad, Pakistan.

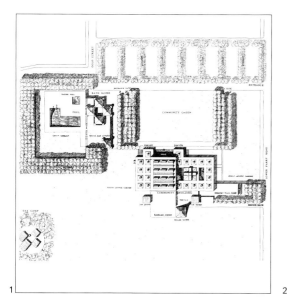

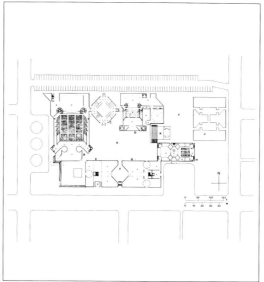

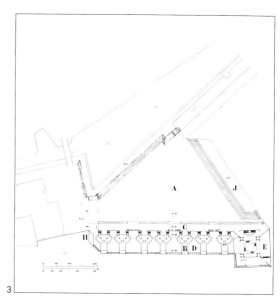

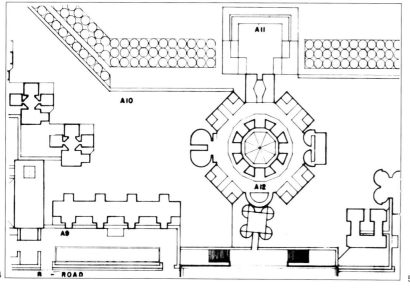

6 Congress Hall, Venice, Italy.
7 Inner Harbor Project, Baltimore, Maryland.
8 Franklin Delano Roosevelt Memorial, Roosevelt Island, New York.
9 Family-Planning Center, Kathmandu, Nepal.
10 Pocono Art Center, Pennsylvania.

6

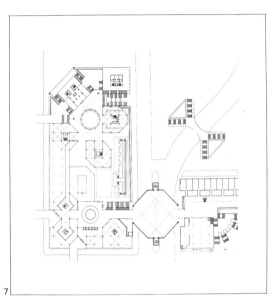

7

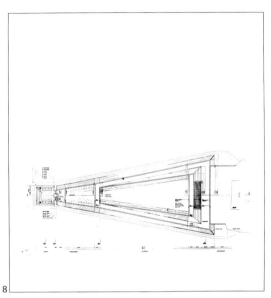

8

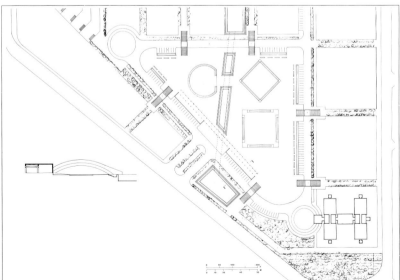

9

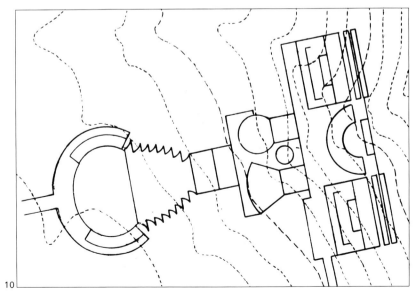

10

1 Trenton Jewish Community Center
Trenton, New Jersey

1954—1959

A community center for various social activities, a gymnasium, and a bath house constituted the original program; only the bath house is built.

Structure and activities are integrated. The community center is a composition of three spatial units: 10' × 10', 10' × 20', and 20' × 20'. This allows each activity to have a structural identity of its own, depending upon the space it needs. This is further emphasized by the roof, which is made of repeatable units.

All these elements are present in the bath house — the support facility for the swimming pool — which consists of four spatial units grouped around a court. Each unit in turn has four "servant" spaces at the corners.

The materials are concrete masonry units and timber.

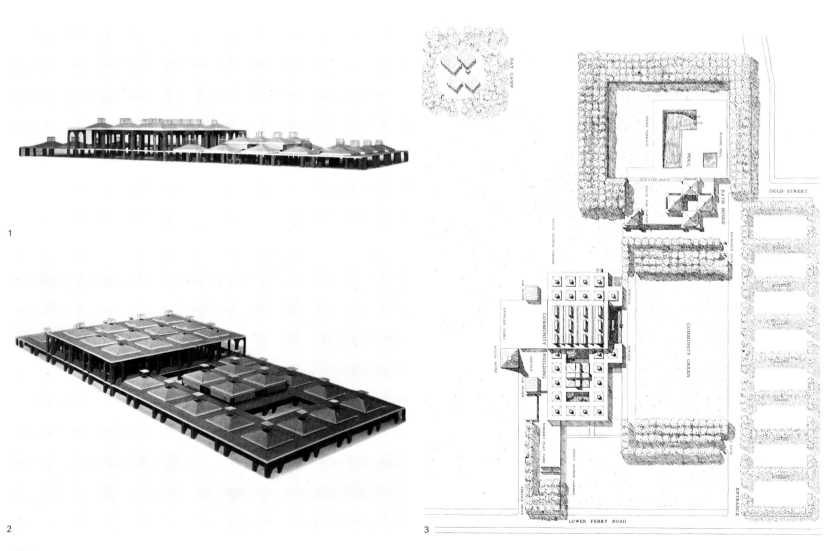

1

2

3

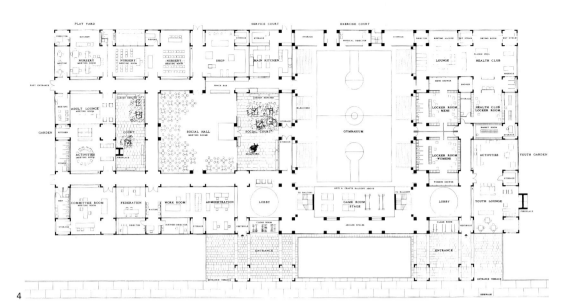

1/2 Models – Community Building.
3   Site plan.
4   Plan – Community Building.
5/6 Perspective sketches, Community Building.

4

5

6

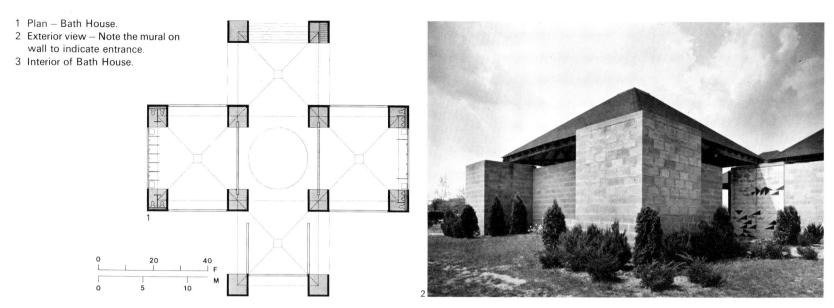

1 Plan – Bath House.
2 Exterior view – Note the mural on wall to indicate entrance.
3 Interior of Bath House.

0   20   40
              F
0 5 10
              M

2 Fort Wayne Fine Arts Center Fort Wayne, Indiana

Project 1961–1964

The original program included the following elements, to be located in one group: 1) Philharmonic Hall, 2) Theater, 3) Museum, 4) School of Art, 5) Dormitories, 6) Art Alliance, and 7) Parking Garage.

The first scheme contained all these elements; however, it went through a radical transformation when subjected to an intense analysis of both the nature of the organization as well as the internal character of the elements themselves. In the process, some of the original elements were dropped while new ones found their place.

A series of models shows the transformation of the initial scheme.

1 Philharmonic Hall
2 Theater
3 Museum
4 School of Art
5 Dormitories
6 Art Alliance
7 Garage
8 School of Ballet
9 Amphitheater

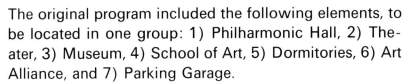

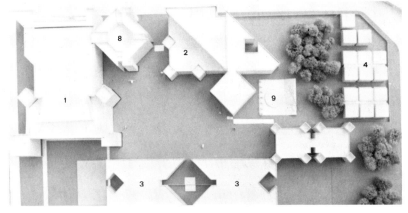

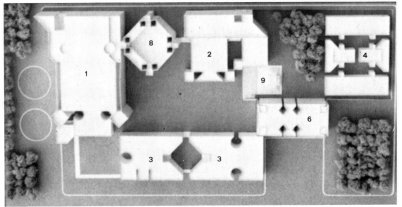

In the latest scheme, a courtyard — previously absent — provides the character of the entire complex, while a way of making light available via lightwells permeates the architecture of all the buildings.

Site plan.

A Court of the entrances

B Philharmonic Hall
1 Entrance
2 Lobby
3 Stair
4 Chamber
5 Stage
6 Workshop

C Philharmonic Annex
1 Green-room
2 Actors' entrance
3 Lobby
4 Public entrance
5 Star dressing

D Civic Theater
1 Entrance
2 Lobby
3 Chamber
4 Stage
5 Workshop (Dressing below)
6 Actors' entrance
7 Experimental theater
8 Entrance
9 Court

E Historical Museum

F Garden

G Art Museum
1 Entrance
2 Gallery
3 Service
4 Offices

H Reception Center
1 Entrance
2 Hall
3 Stair
4 Lounge
5 Meeting-room
6 Committee-room

J School of Art

K Amphitheater

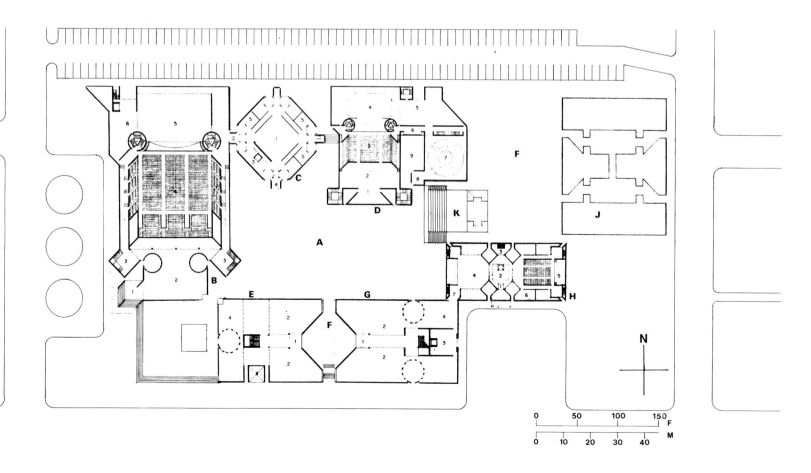

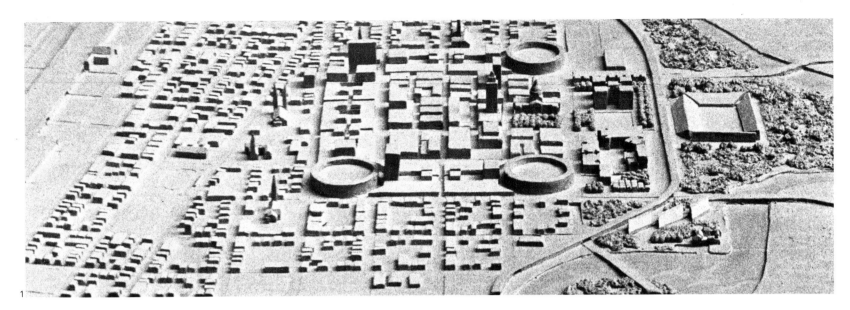

1 Kahn proposed a design for the center of Fort Wayne. The three circular buildings are parking and shopping centers reminiscent of the ones in Philadelphia. The new Fine Arts Center is located on the right, with a sports center across the railroad track.
2 Bird's-eye view looking north.
3 Model of the final scheme. The School of Art is in the foreground.

Theater of Performing Arts
Fort Wayne, Indiana

1966–1973

The search for the institution of theater and its essential nature is evident in the several stages of the project before it took its final form, in which three primary elements became clearly articulated.

These elements are: 1) ''The Violin'' – the stage and auditorium chamber, 2) ''The Violin Case'' – the public lobby and galleries surrounding the former, and 3) ''The Actors' House.'' A separate workshop unit sits beside the stage house. The articulation of these elements is carried through in the construction. The chamber is built with a system of folded walls of concrete, while the surrounding lobbies and the Actors' House are built with masonry construction. The theater seats 800 spectators.

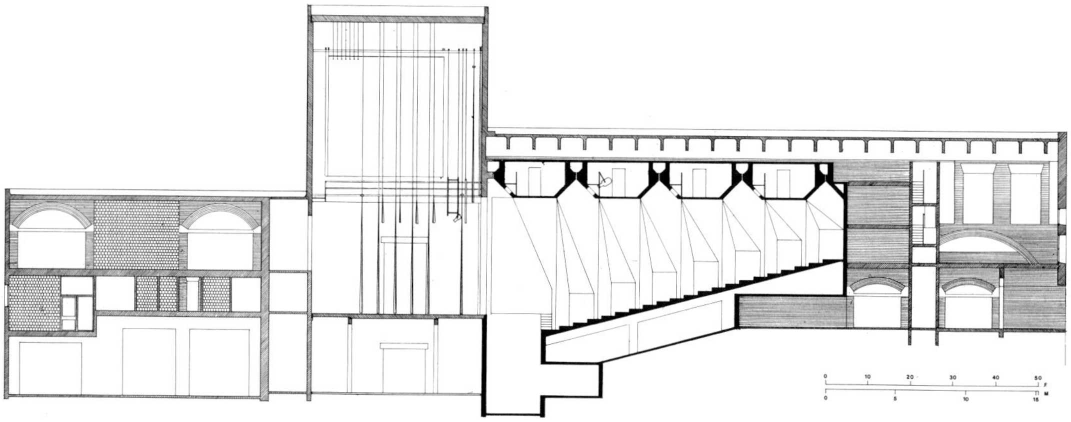

Longitudinal section.

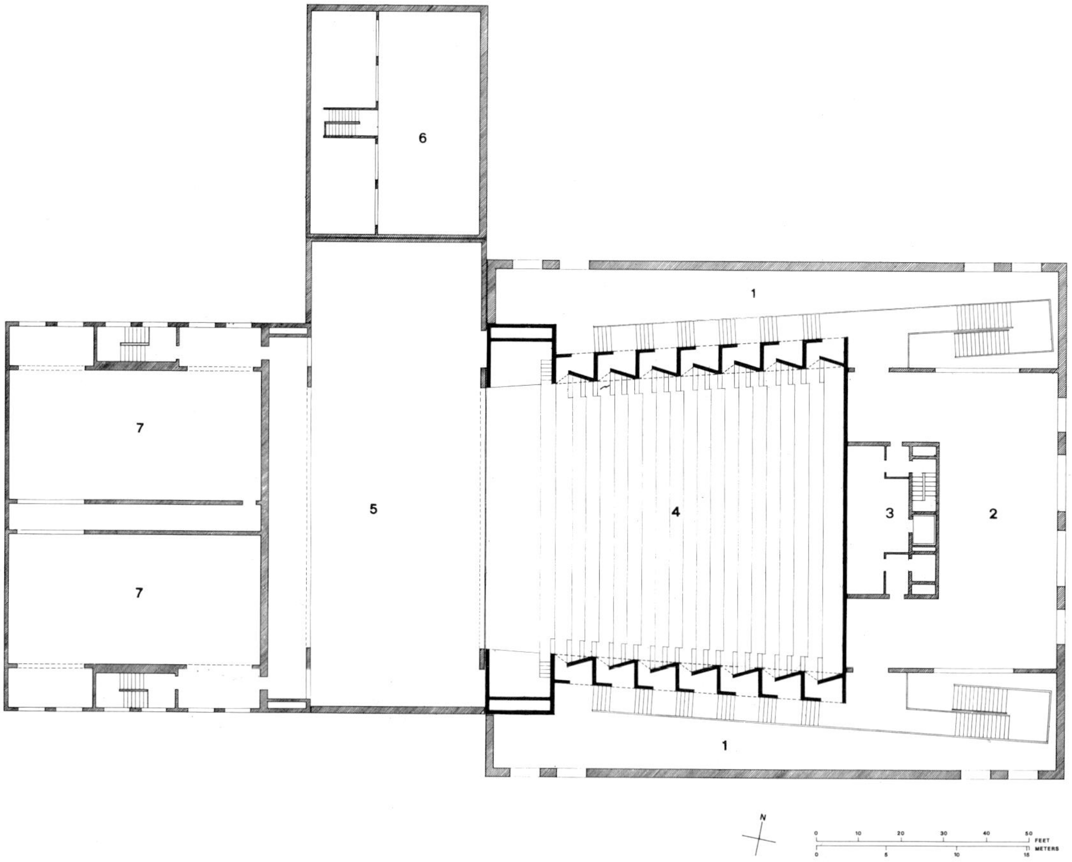

Upper-floor plan.

1 Lobby below
2 Banquet hall
3 Service
4 Chamber
5 Stage
6 Workshop
7 Rehearsal rooms

"The court of the entrances." Looking towards the theater.

Site plan.

1 School of Fine Arts	2 Theater of Performing Arts 3 Philharmonic Hall	4 Philharmonic Annex 5 Art Gallery	6 Art Alliance 7 Court of Entrances	8 Garden 9 Lawn

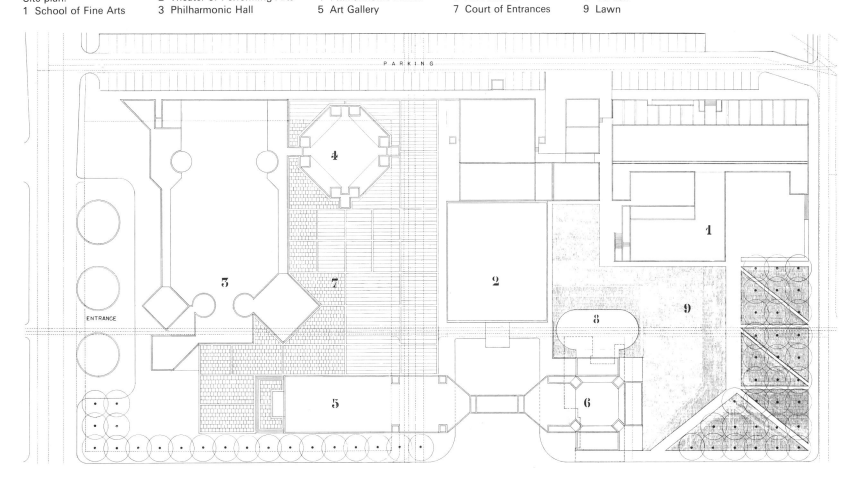

122

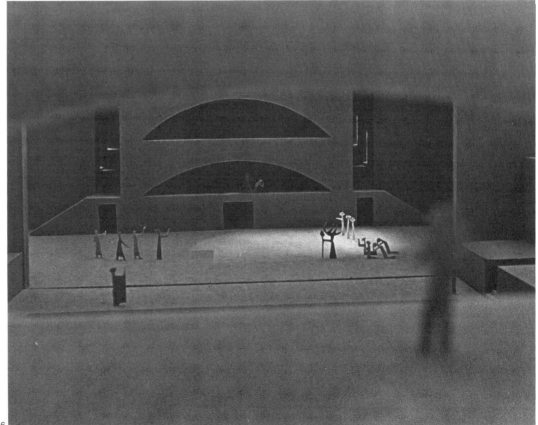

1 View of the entrance.
2 Side lobby.
3 Interior of the chamber.
4 Entrance foyer.
5/6 Study models of an earlier scheme showing the chamber and the stage.

123

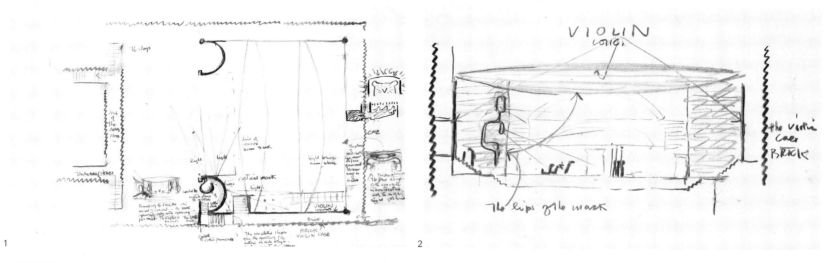

1

2

3

1/2 Sketch plan and section explaining the concept.
3/4 The Banquet Hall.
5 The Chamber. The triangular arch behind the stage leads to the actors' house.

3 "Interama," Inter-American Community Florida

Project 1964–1967

Site plan.

A Ceremonial plaza
B National houses
C Promenade
D Gardens
E Exhibition building
H Tea house
J Amphitheater

As the name implies, this project was an attempt to bring together all the Pan American countries for cultural, technological and academic exchanges. A team of distinguished American architects was brought together to participate in designing what Kahn called "one of the smaller versions of the League of Nations emerging in different parts of the world". There the technological know-how of one nation would be made available to another, and students from each nation would live and work together, exchanging ideas and the ways of their people.

The office of Louis Kahn was entrusted to design the national "houses" and the "Hospitality Center." Each participating nation had a "house" for its representatives to live in during their stay there and a meeting house for the entire community.

The structures are designed in reinforced concrete to resist earthquakes, and the materials are intended to be left exposed.

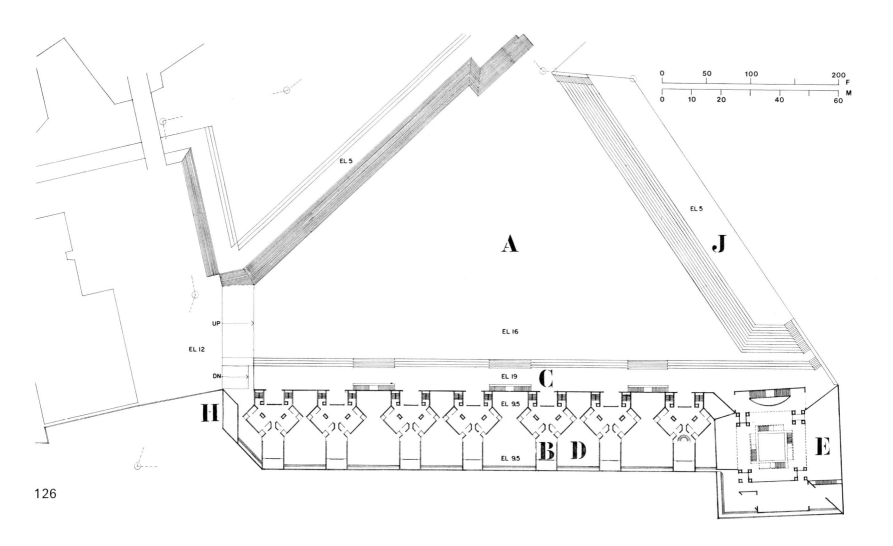

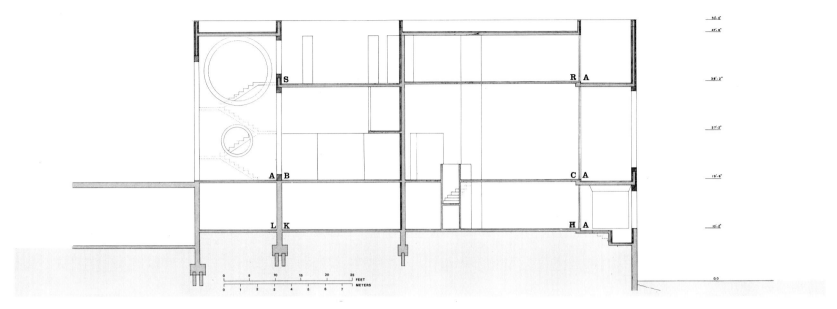

Section through the National houses.

A Porch
B Hall
C Reception
D Library lounge
E Office reception
F Pantry

G Toilets
H Director's living-room
I Master bedroom
K Kitchen
L Mechanical
M Servant

N Storage
O Janitor
P Students' bedroom
Q Students' bathroom
R Students' living-room
S Garden.

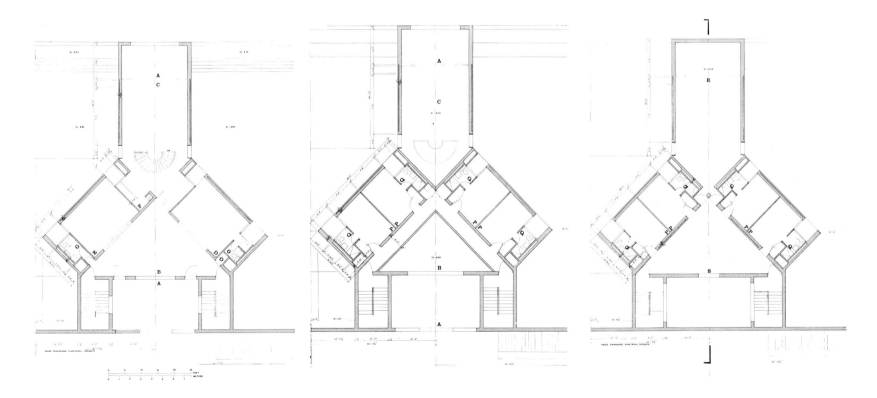

Plan at plaza level.

Plan at second level.

Plan at third level.

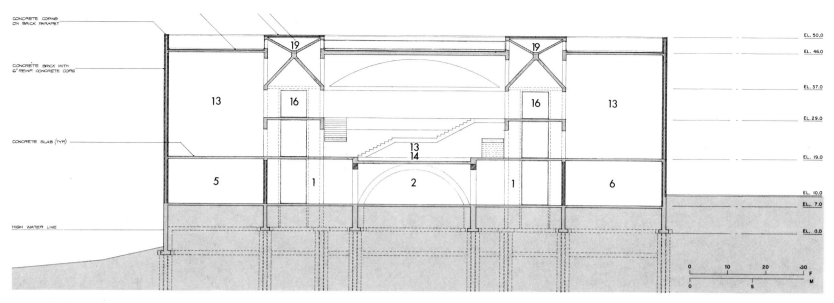

Section C-C.

1 Dining	8 Service entrance	15 Light wells
2 Bar	9 Coats	16 Exhibition
3 Dining terrace	10 Parking	17 Office
4 Toilets	11 Service ramp	18 Machine-room
5 Kitchen	12 Entrance porch	19 Plenum
6 Workshop	13 Exhibition	
7 Loading	14 Auditorium	

Basement floor.

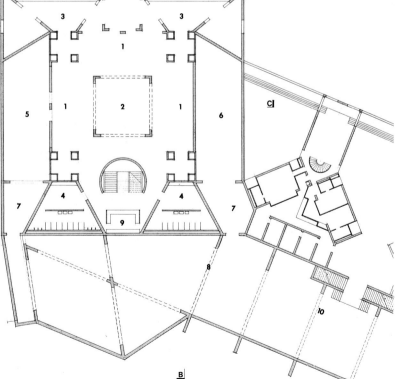

Plan at plaza level.

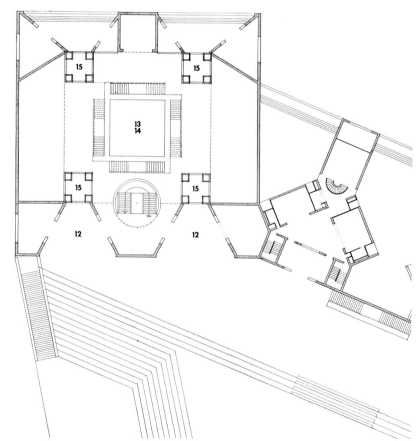

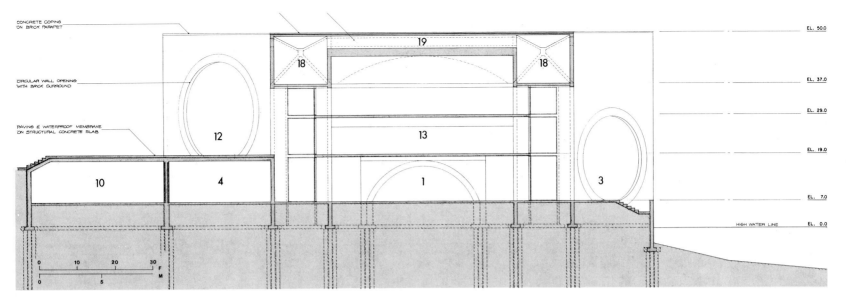

Section B-B.

Plan at mezzanine level.

Plan at roof.

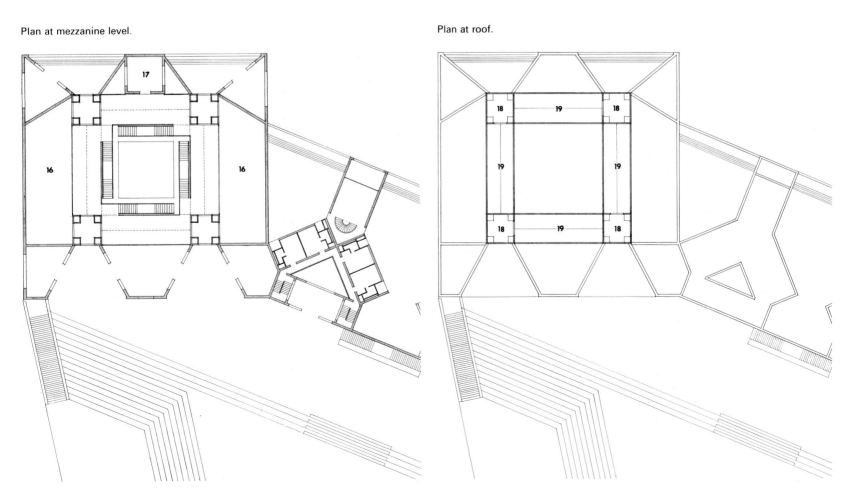

129

4 "Banglanagar," Capital Complex of Bangladesh Dacca, Bangladesh

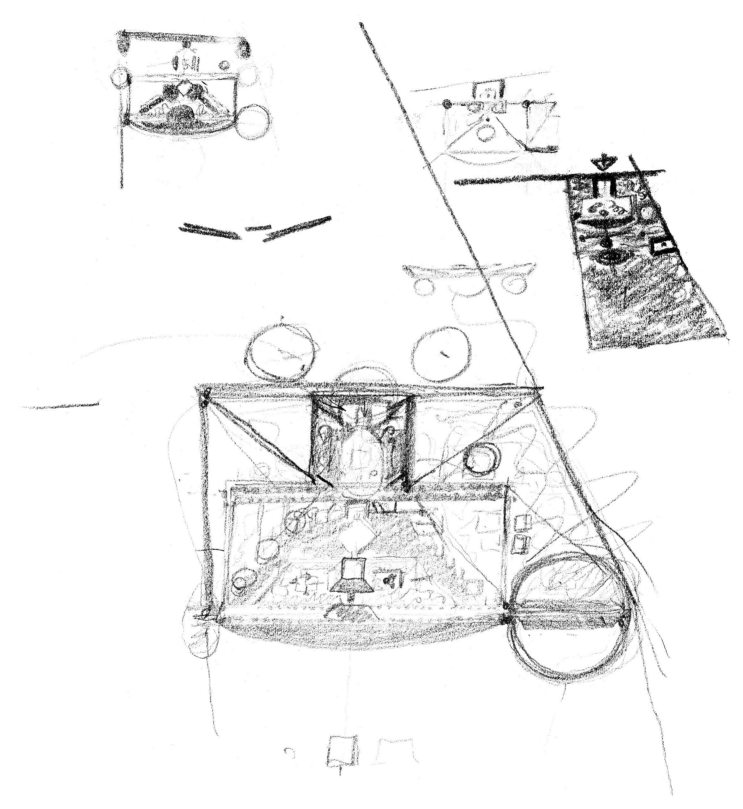

A page from the sketchbook shows the early formation of the plan.

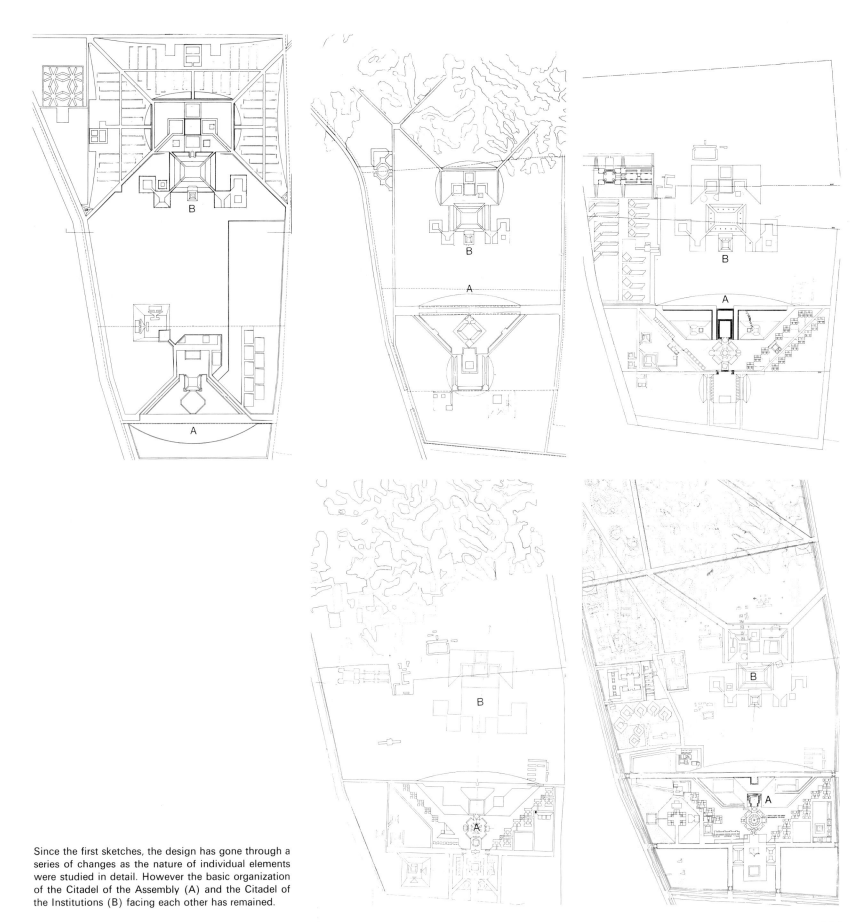

Since the first sketches, the design has gone through a series of changes as the nature of individual elements were studied in detail. However the basic organization of the Citadel of the Assembly (A) and the Citadel of the Institutions (B) facing each other has remained.

131

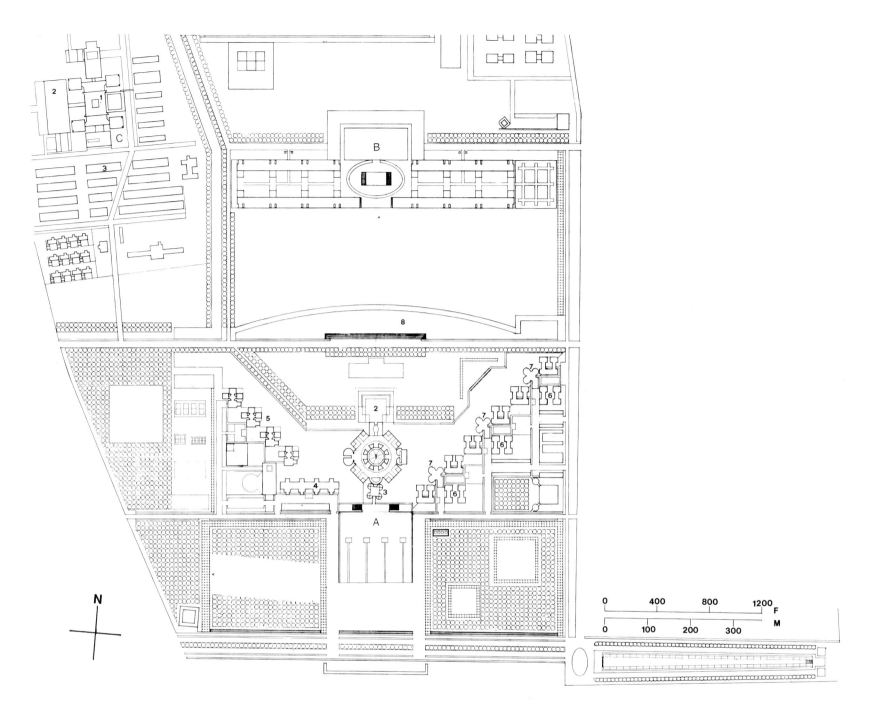

Site plan

A Citadel of the Assembly
1 Assembly building
2 Presidential Square
3 Prayer Hall
4 Hostels for Ministers
5 Hostels for Secretaries
6 Hostels for members of the Assembly
7 Dining halls
8 Lake

B Secretariat

C Hospital complex
1 Hospital
2 Out-patient department
3 Staff housing

Model of the complex.

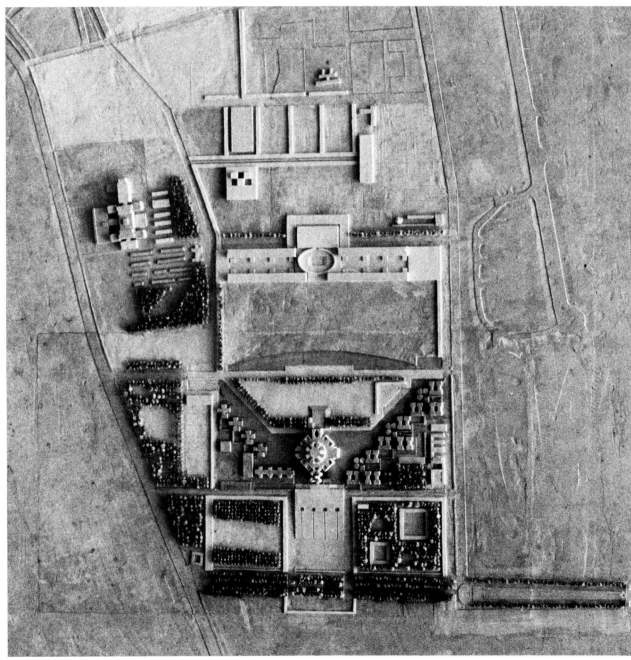

Model of the Capital complex. In the north of the Citadel of the Assembly is the new secretariat.

A view of the Assembly as it appears from Dacca.

An aerial view of the Assembly under construction. The buildings in the foreground at the right are hostels for secretaries. Above left are the hostels for the members of the Assembly and the dining halls. The hostels for ministers run from the right middle to right below.

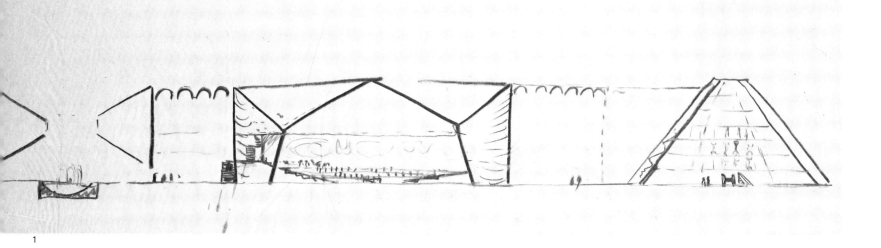

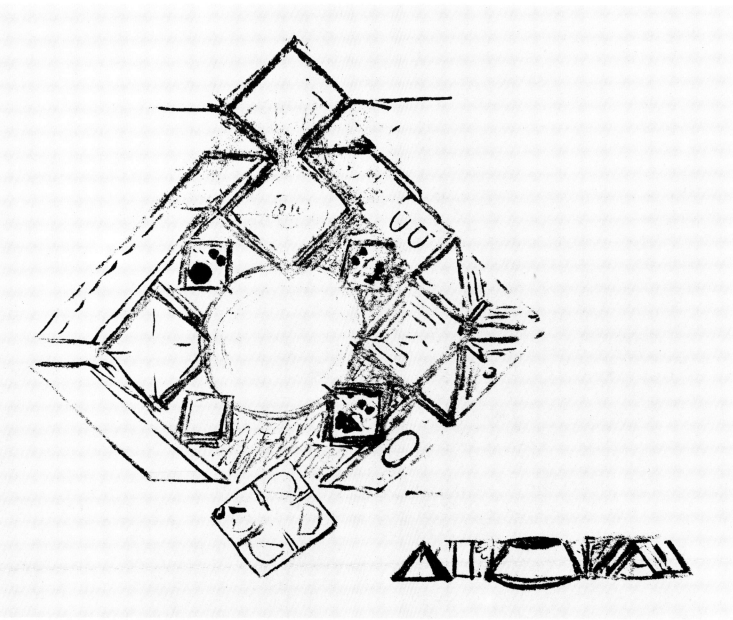

136

3

1 An early sketch section through the Assembly. The Prayer Hall is on the right.
2 Further development of the plan and section.
3/4 Elevation studies — Assembly Building.

4

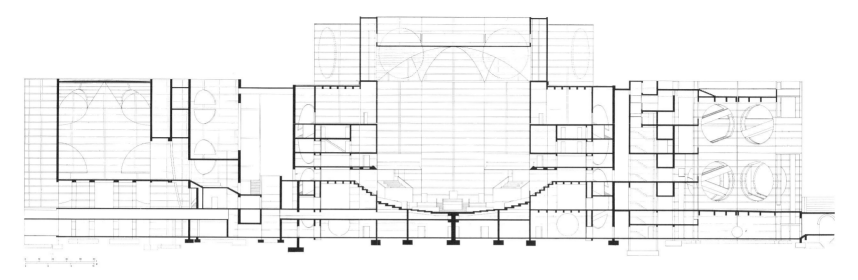

Section through Assembly looking west. The Prayer Hall is on the left.

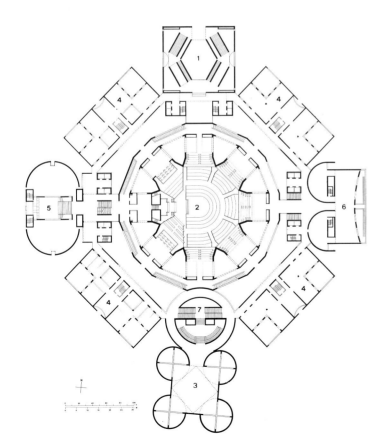

Plan of the Assembly.

1 Entrance hall
2 Assembly Chamber
3 Prayer Hall
4 Offices
5 Ministers' Lounge
6 Dining and Recreation
7 Ablution Court

View of Assembly seen through secretaries' quarters.

The Assembly building – North view. As foreground to the strongly geometric buildings Kahn wanted nothing but a great carpet of grass.

Interior of the entrance hall. The white marble strips mark the pour joints in the concrete walls.

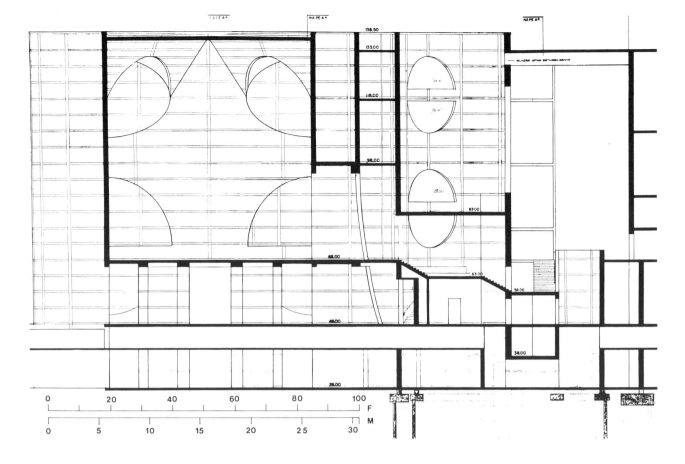

Section through Prayer Hall.

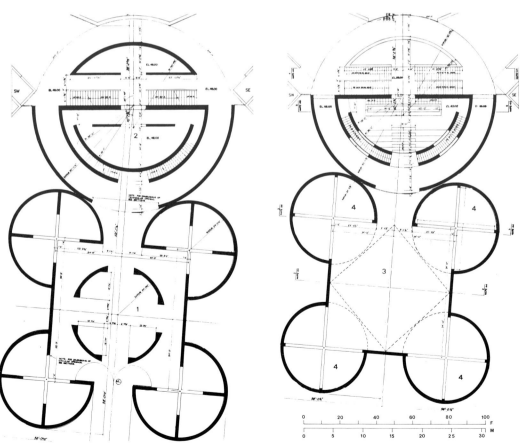

Plans — Prayer Hall.
Exterior left: Plan at level 48'.
Left: Plan at level 68'.

1 Entrance
2 Ablution Court
3 Prayer-room
4 Open light well

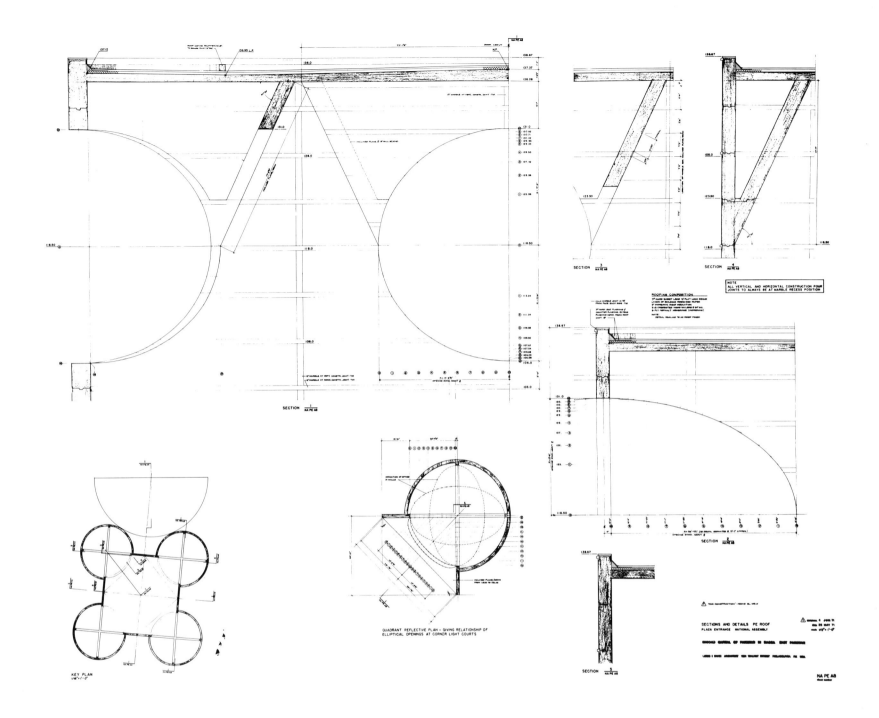

Construction details for Prayer-Hall roof and openings.

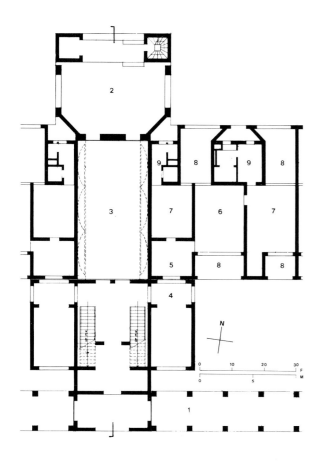

Plan and section – Hostels for Ministers.

1 Covered archade
2 Porch
3 Hall
4 Vestibule
5 Entrance
6 Living-room
7 Bedroom
8 Veranda
9 Bathroom

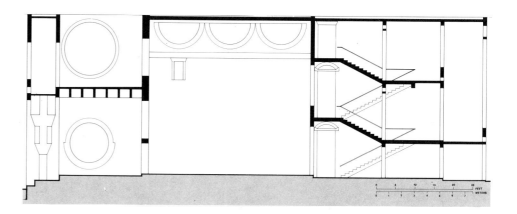

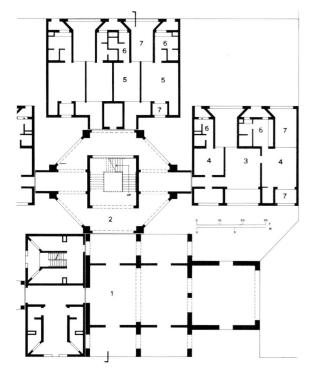

Plan and section – Hostel for Secretaries.

1 Entrance porch
2 Stair hall
3 Living-room
4 Bedroom
5 Living/bedroom
6 Bathroom
7 Veranda

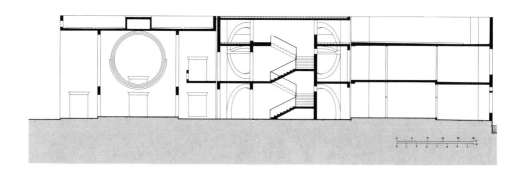

Secretaries' hostels — View from the lake.

South view of Ministers' hostel.

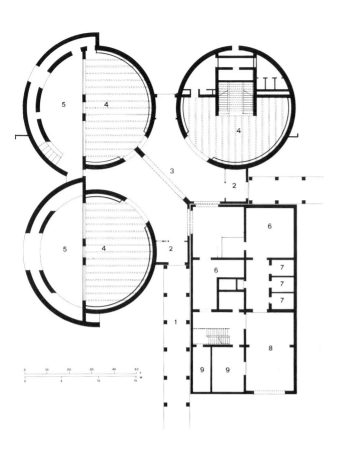

Plan and section through dining hall for members of National Assembly.

1 Covered walkway
2 Vestibule
3 Lobby
4 Lounge
5 Garden court
6 Dry storage
7 Refrigeration
8 Service court
9 Utilities

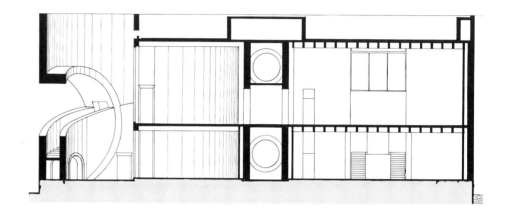

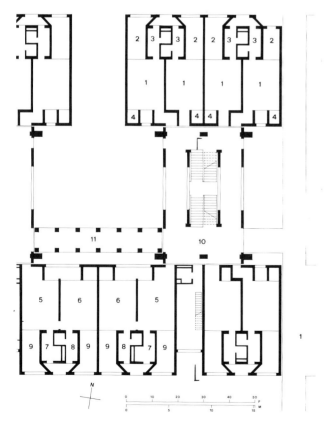

Hostel for members of National Assembly.

One-room unit:
1 Living/bedroom
2 Porch
3 Bathroom
4 Closet

Two-room unit:
5 Living-room
6 Bedroom
7 Kitchen
8 Bathroom
9 Porch
10 Stair gallery
11 Covered walkway

Section through stair gallery.

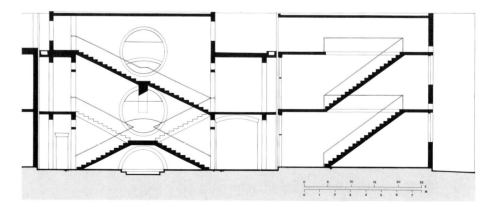

View of the dining hall from across the lake.

Hostels for members of National Assembly.

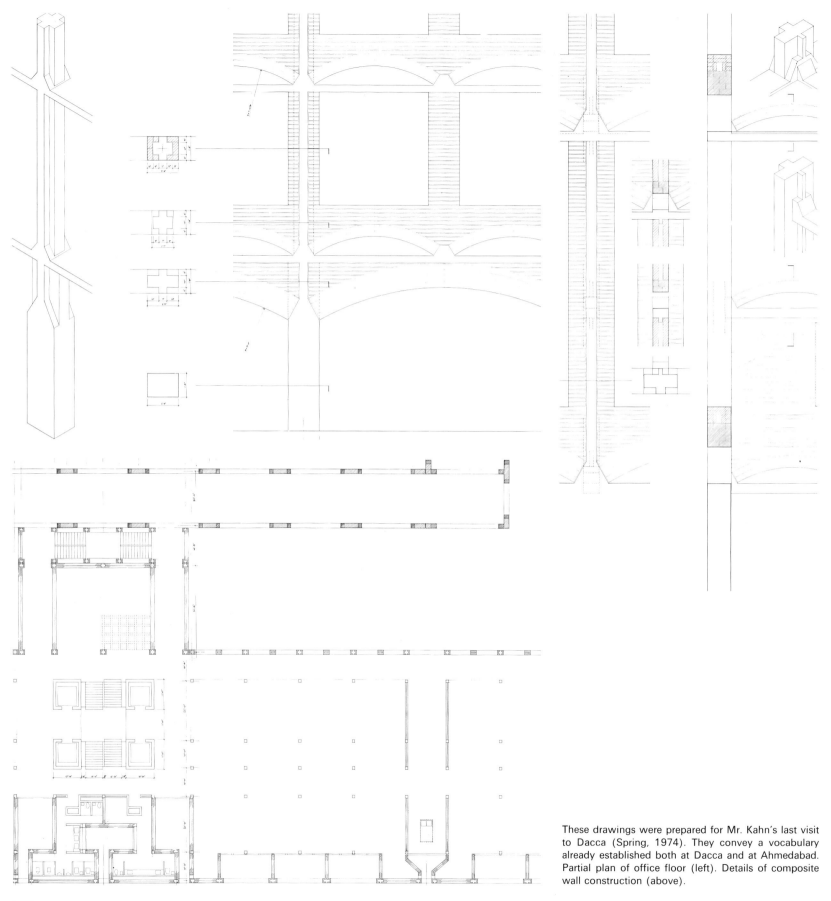

These drawings were prepared for Mr. Kahn's last visit to Dacca (Spring, 1974). They convey a vocabulary already established both at Dacca and at Ahmedabad. Partial plan of office floor (left). Details of composite wall construction (above).

148

Hostels for secretaries. View from the Assembly building. The brick harmonizes with the scenery.

5 Capital Complex of Western Pakistan
Islamabad, Pakistan

Project 1965

In addition to Dacca, in East Pakistan, the government of Pakistan wanted a capital in its western division. The site chosen was the magnificent foothills of the Hindukusk and Karakorum mountains of the northwest provinces. The office of Louis Kahn was asked to design the government center, consisting of the Assembly, the Supreme Court, the Museum of Islamic Histories, and the Presidential Mansion, including the president's offices.

The visitor approaches the capital complex via a sunken highway which brings him to a ceremonial square, defined by the Assembly building, the Museum, and the hill on top of which sits the Presidential Mansion. The Supreme Court is on the other side of the highway. The Presidential Mansion itself is approached directly through a ramp, which also connects different levels of the Museum. Kahn created an artificial lake, joining the three hills behind the Mansion.

Model of the second version.

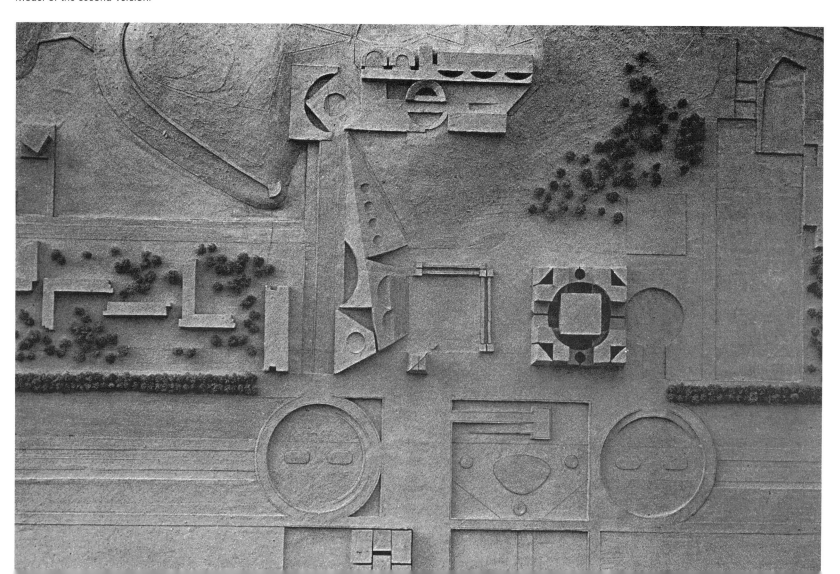

Section through the site.

1 Presidential Mansion
2 Council of Islamic Studies
3 Monument

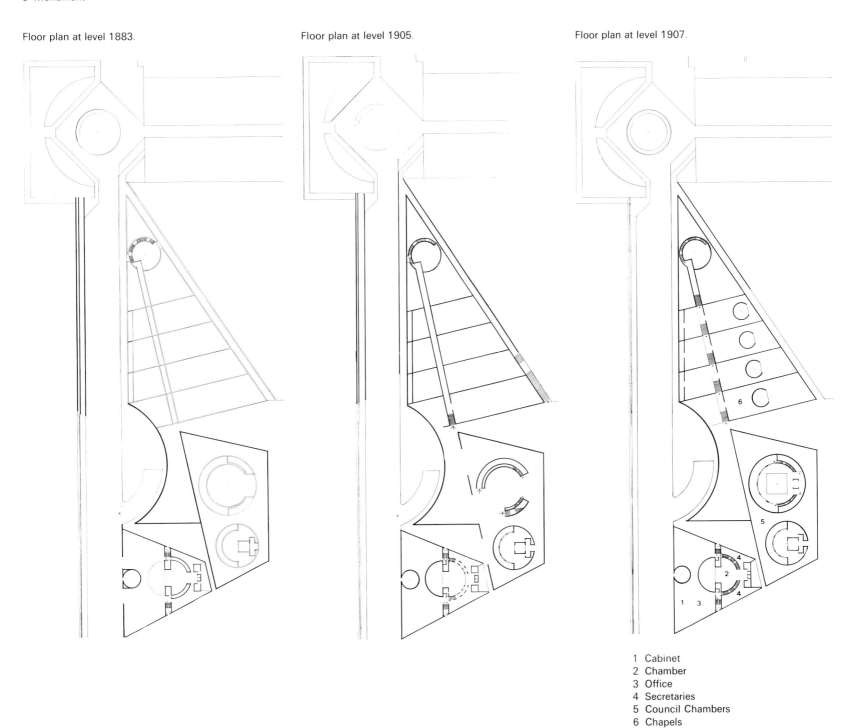

Floor plan at level 1883.

Floor plan at level 1905.

Floor plan at level 1907.

1 Cabinet
2 Chamber
3 Office
4 Secretaries
5 Council Chambers
6 Chapels

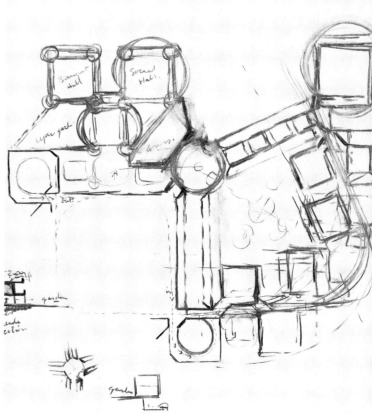

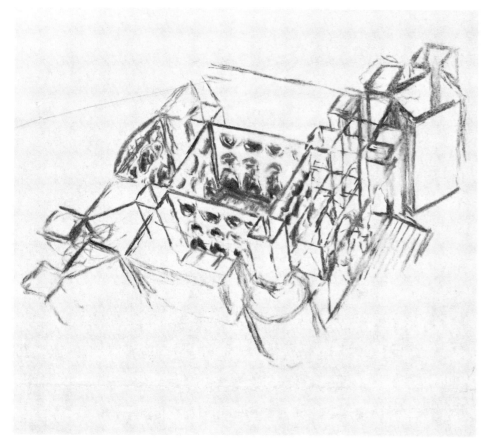

Early studies for the Presidential Mansion. Site plan (above left), plan (above), isometric sketch (left), bird's-eye view of the Presidential Mansion (right). The Monument Square and part of the Assembly Hall are in the foreground.

Model of the intermediate version.

Site plan – Final version.

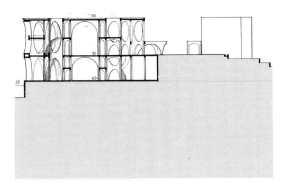

Section 4-4.

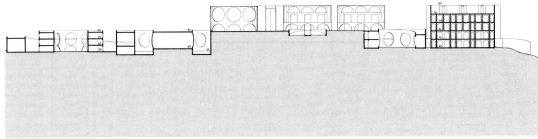

Section 2-2.

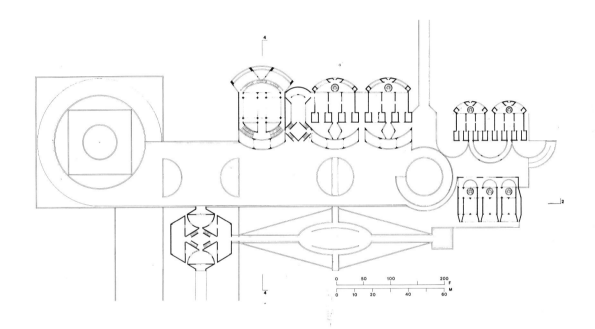

Plan at level 90.

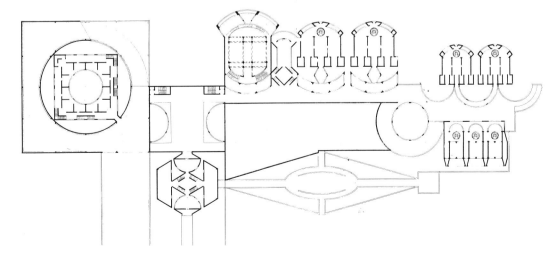

Plan at level 60.

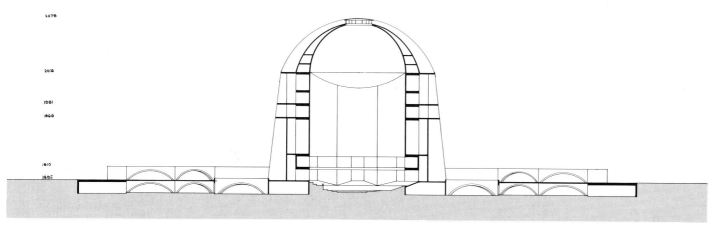

Section A-A.

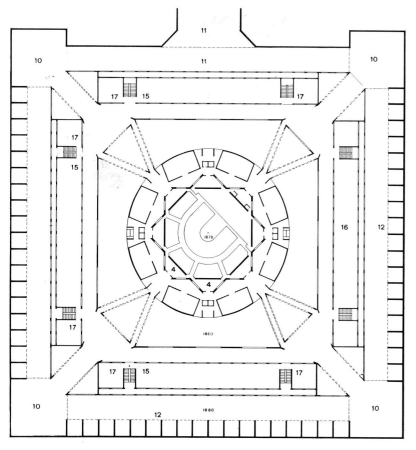

Plan at lower level.

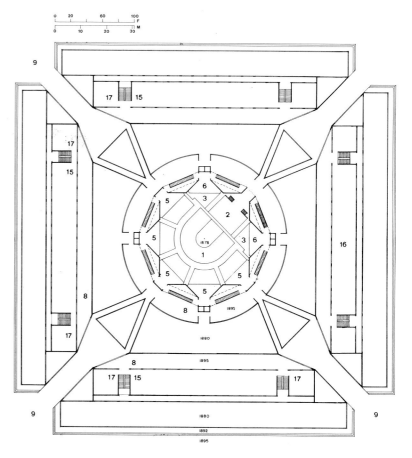

Plan at entrance level.

1 Assembly Chamber
2 Speaker
3 Distinguished visitors' gallery
4 Members' anterooms
5 Public galleries
6 Press galleries
7 Television
8 Public promenade
9 Public entrances
10 Members' entrances
11 Car drive
12 Garages
15 Offices
16 Reception wing
17 Utilities and toilets

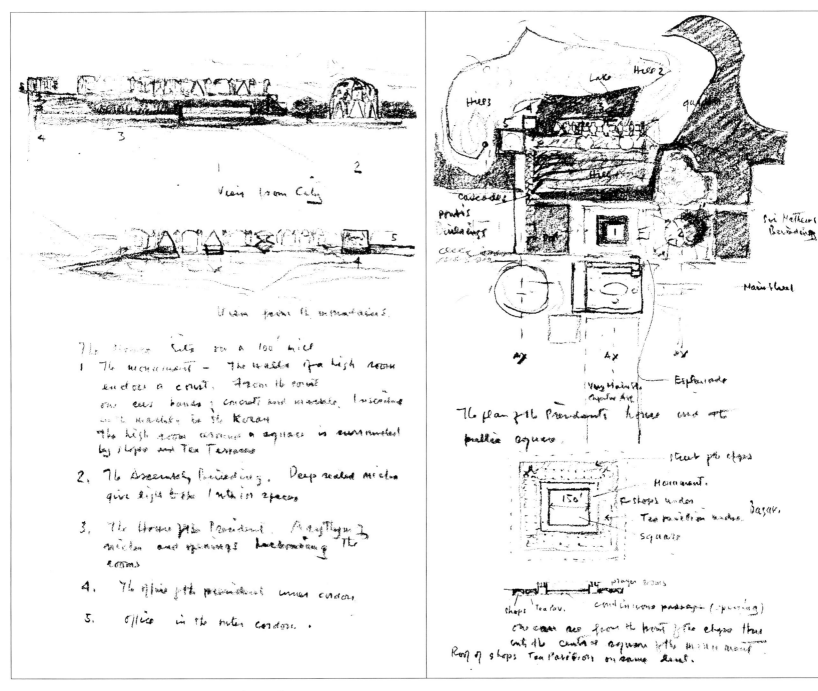

Two pages from the sketch book. Plan and elevation studies.

6 Memorial to Six Million Jews New York City

Project 1967–1969

The Committee of Art decided that the memorial should express the meaning of the event without pictorial representation. Louis Kahn agreed and also felt that the memorial should have a non-accusatory character. He chose glass as the material to express this because, unlike stone, it casts transparent shadows.

Six glass piers, each 10′ × 10′ × 11′ high, form an enclave for the central chapel, also of the same dimension but hollow and open to the sky. The spaces between the piers have dimension equal to that of the piers. The piers are made with solid blocks of glass, placed one above the other and interlocking without the use of mortar. The top of each pier is sealed with a thin layer of lead set into specially designed joints.

All seven piers stand on a granite base 66 feet square.

The memorial is situated at the southern tip of Manhattan Island — one of the points of entry into America.

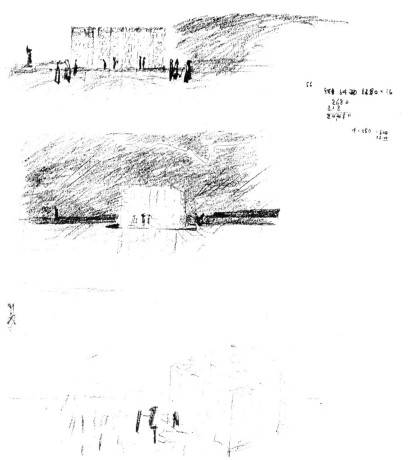

Two pages from Kahn's sketch book.

Study model. In the background is the old wall of Battery Park.

Model of the final version.

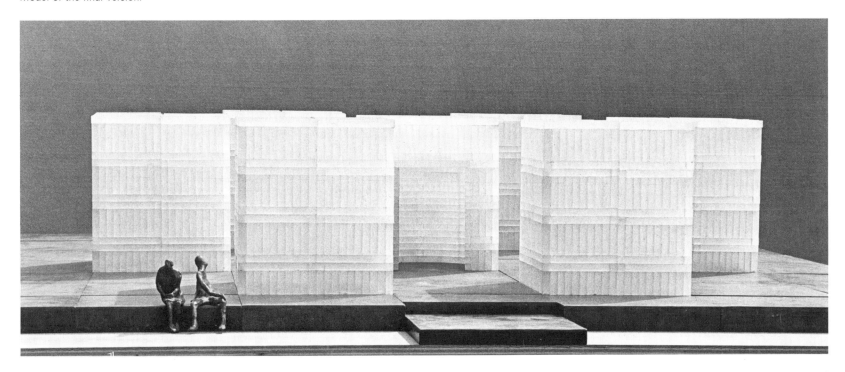

7 Congress Hall
Venice, Italy

Project 1969
Structural Engineer: August Komendant

In a city of perpetual confrontation between land and sea, Kahn's new Congress Hall is designed on the theme of friendly confrontation between ideas or attitudes, out of which new institutions emerge.

Acknowledging the difficulty of building on land in the city, Kahn conceived Congress Hall as a bridge, 460 feet long, 100 feet wide, and 78 feet high, supported by four massive concrete pylons which contain elevators and stairs. The curvature of the meeting hall is gentle in order to retain the sense that it is really a street-like piazza, gently sloping — a civic theater.

The main hall seats 2500 people and can be divided into two sections, for a capacity of 1500 people. The upper level contains three separate halls, each crowned with a dome 70 feet in diameter. The domes are made of glass and stainless steel rings and are covered on the outside with lead.

Site model.

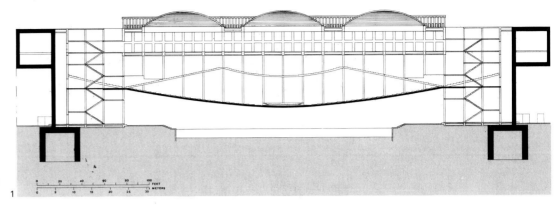

1 Longitudinal section.
2 Basin entrances.
3 Plan of Congress Hall
4 Diagrammatic cable positions of the bridge structure
 of the Congress Hall.

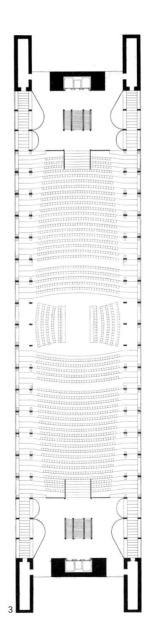

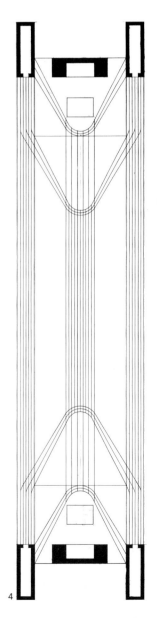

161

1
2

1 Model of the first scheme at the Biennale site.
2 Model, perspective view.
3 Site plan of the second scheme.

3

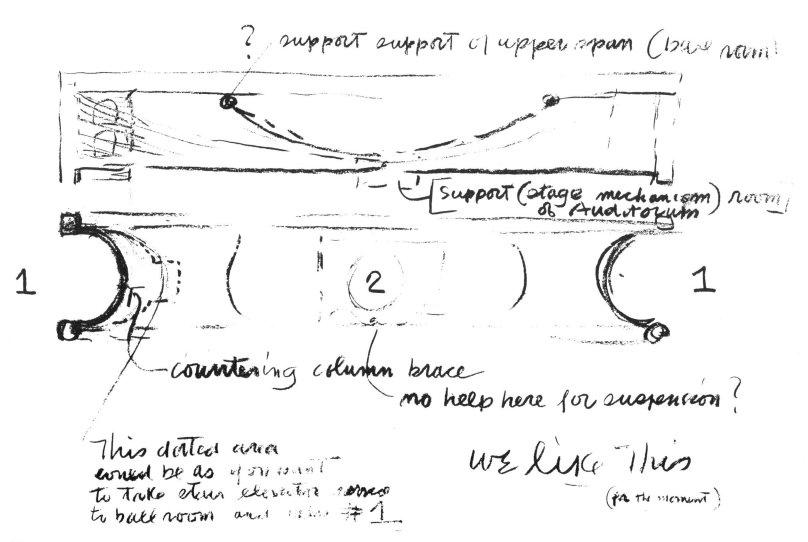

? support support of upper span (bare room)

support (stage mechanism) room of Auditorium

1   ((2   )   )   1

countering column brace
no help here for suspension?

This dotted area would be as you want to take stair elevator access to ball room and also #1

we like this
(for the moment)

Schematic sketches.

Hollow metal and ceramic lion of St. Mark at the entrances to the assembly. Walking through the body of the sculpture over the bridge of its head and wings

Hollow metal and ceramic lion of St. Mark at the entrances to the Assembly. Walking through the body of the sculpture over the bridge of its head and wings.

8 Inner Harbor Project Baltimore, Maryland

Project 1971–1973

The project is situated on the Baltimore waterfront and contains both commercial and civic activities.

A high water table prompted the decision to raise the buildings on a podium. Kahn called this podium "a new contour" in the city. He felt that this podium must have a sense of place, an identifiable character.

The buildings are shaped and placed so as not to make an impenetrable wall towards the street.

Construction is in the American vernacular of concrete frame with central utility core and offices or living units around.

Perspective drawing looking south-west.

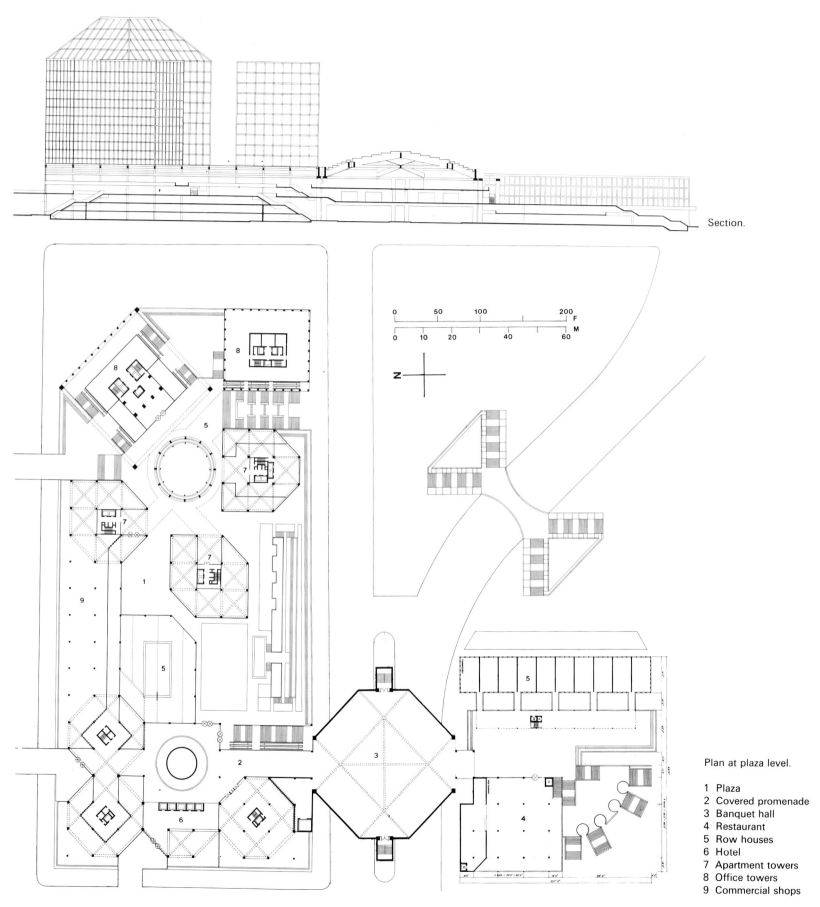

Section.

Plan at plaza level.

1 Plaza
2 Covered promenade
3 Banquet hall
4 Restaurant
5 Row houses
6 Hotel
7 Apartment towers
8 Office towers
9 Commercial shops

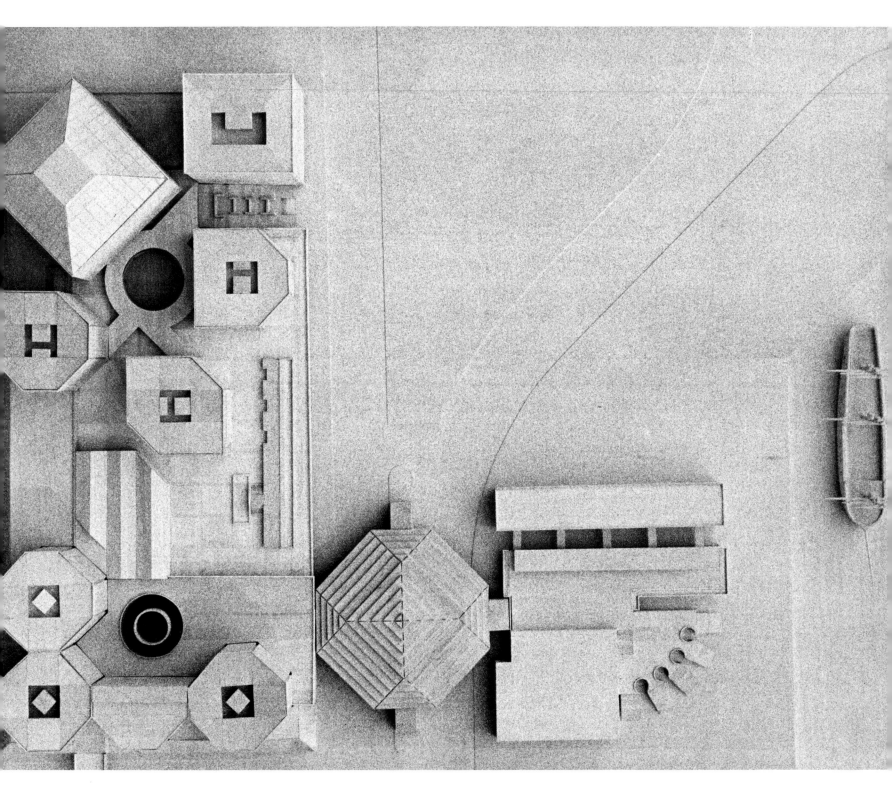

Site model.

View from south.

Entrance from south.

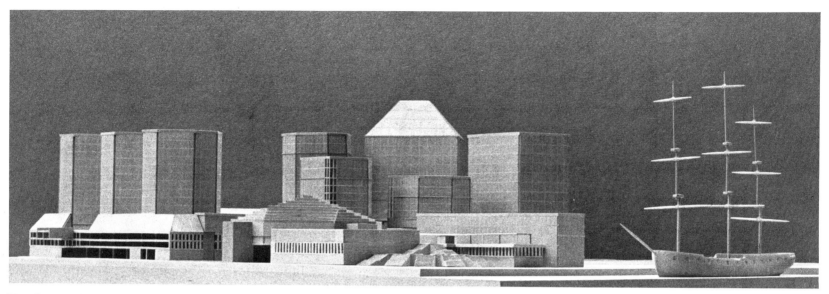

View from south-west.

View from north.

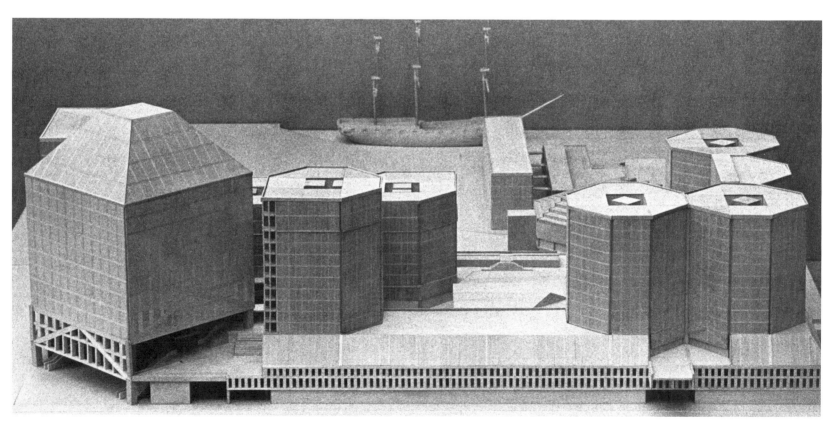

View of the plaza. The hotel is in the background.

The Banquet Hall.

9 Family Planning Center
Kathmandu, Nepal

1970   Under construction

In 1970, His Majesty's Government asked Kahn to design the Family Planning Center. A large triangular piece of land outside the old city walls and near the old palace is set aside to consolidate a number of public institutions. The new Family Planning Center is a part of this. Kahn recommended a plan for the entire area. Each institution would be placed in a rectangular plot on the periphery, separated by pedestrian bridges, which also connect the outer edge with the inner raised platform. Vehicular entrances are provided from below this platform. Kahn was fond of calling this place "the availability square."

The Family Planning Center occupies one of the rectangular plots. The building is made of load-bearing brick construction.

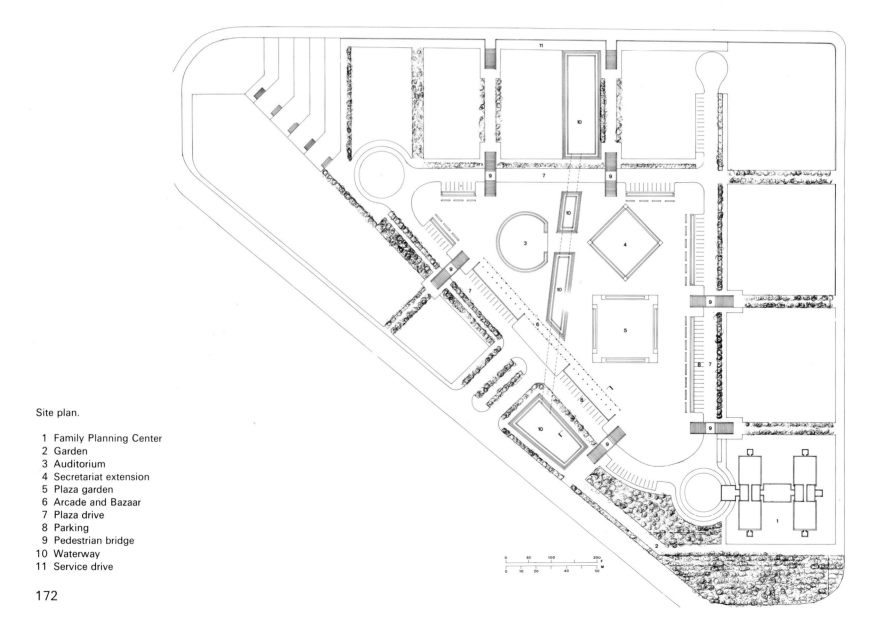

Site plan.

1 Family Planning Center
2 Garden
3 Auditorium
4 Secretariat extension
5 Plaza garden
6 Arcade and Bazaar
7 Plaza drive
8 Parking
9 Pedestrian bridge
10 Waterway
11 Service drive

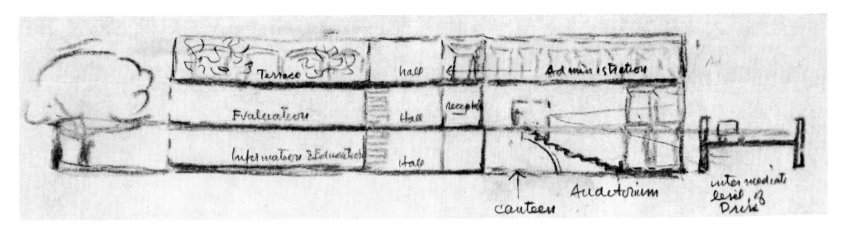

Plan and section studies.

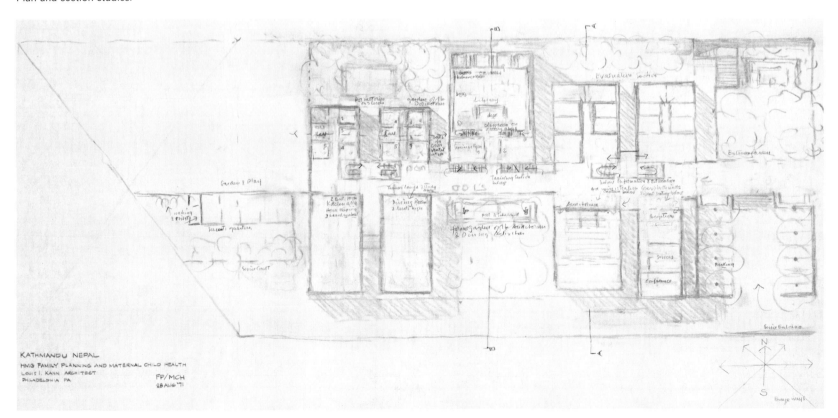

173

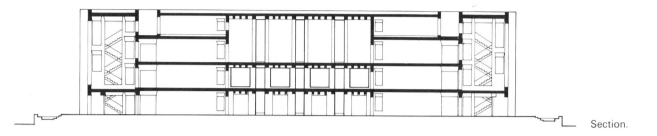

Section.

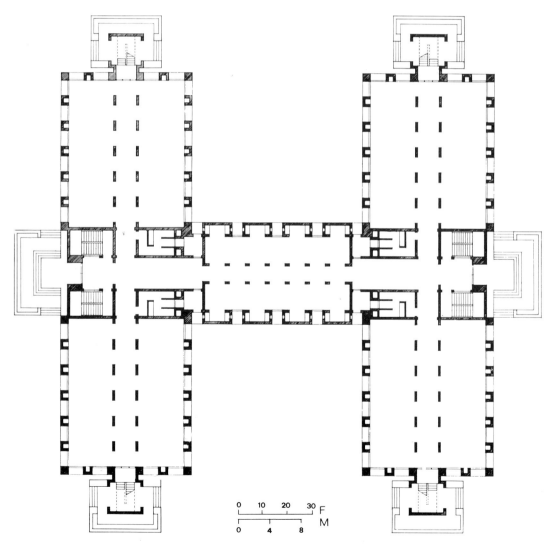

0 10 20 30 F
            M
0   4   8

Plan.

Model, lateral view.

Model – Family Planning Center.

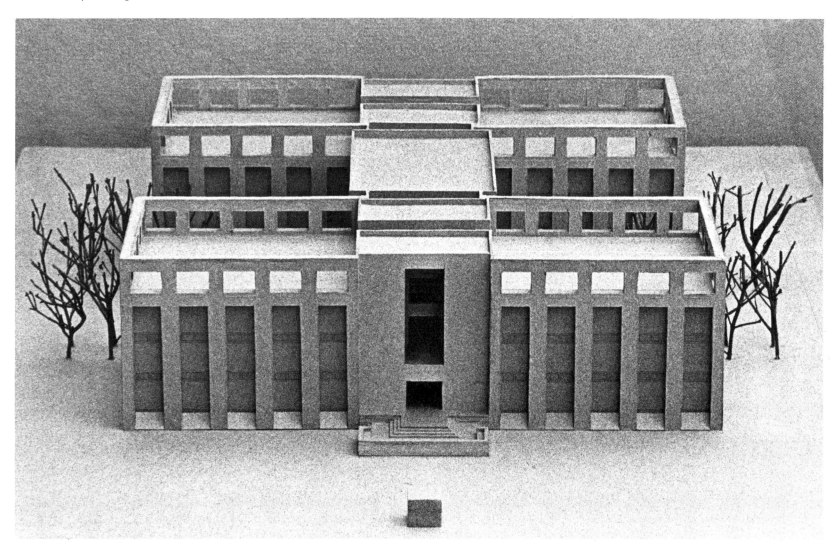

10 Pocono Art Center
Pennsylvania

Project 1973

The Pocono Art Center is conceived as a year-round facility incorporating a Summer Festival of musical and other performing arts together with a summer-winter Academy of Dance, Music, Drama, and the Visual Arts.
Located on a site overlooking the Lehigh River and adjacent to the Francis E. Walter Dam, the Art Center will be close to Philadelphia and New York City.
The Summer Festival will be housed in a partially roofed, partially open-air concert theater seating 3000, with views to the river and forest. Seating for an additional 3000 will be provided on a gently sloping lawn. The

Site model.

large stage house and 80-foot proscenium will accommodate symphony concerts, grand opera, theatrical, and dance productions. A summer practice theater and exhibition gallery together with workshops, food services, entrance kiosks, rest rooms, and hidden parking for 3000 cars will complete the Summer Festival services.

The Academy of Dance, Music, Drama, and the Visual Arts will be housed in year-round structures. These will include two smaller theaters, each with a capacity of 1000 persons, an experimental theater-in-the-round, and an open-to-the-sky summer amphitheater. The Academy workshops, practice rooms, studios and living quarters will be placed in a setting of gardens, fountains and sculpture. The workshops of the Academy and the Summer Festival will interconnect to serve each other as required.

The Academy will function summer and winter, providing chamber music, dance, experimental theater, cinema, and other art forms.

The Governor of the State of Pennsylvania has proposed that the center be named after Louis Kahn.

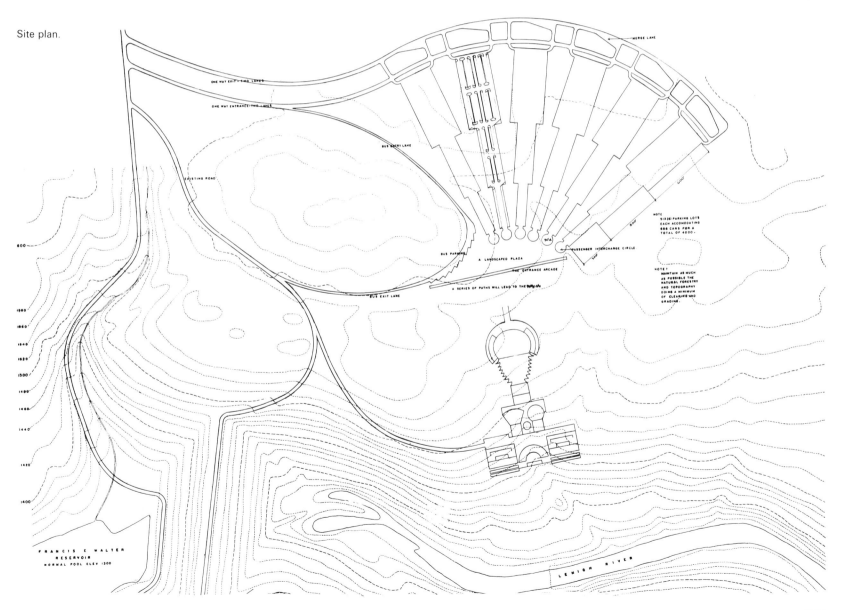

Site plan.

11 Franklin Delano Roosevelt Memorial
Roosevelt Island, New York

1973

The memorial stands at the southern end of the small island now named after the late president.

A "room" and a garden constitute the architecture of the memorial. The "room" is 60 feet square and open to the sky. Two walls define the room. These walls are made with solid blocks of granite 6' × 6' × 12' high. The size is determined by the maximum weight a crane can carry.

A statue of the late president carved out of a granite block sits between the "room" and the garden. The memorial is raised above water level by a stone base.

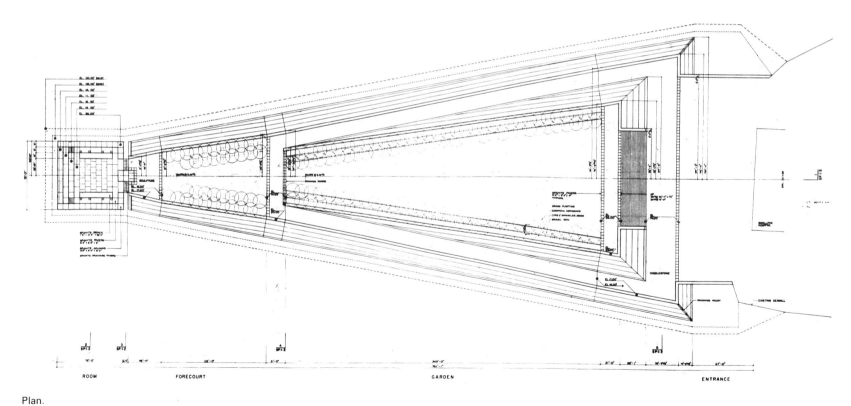

ROOM   FORECOURT   GARDEN   ENTRANCE

Plan.

Model of the complex at the southern end of the island.

Model, in the foreground the "room" open to the sky.

Architecture

Let us move from thought to work. There is a structure to the architecture of Louis Kahn — a structure that conveys his faith in the standards he put for himself as a test of his real independence of mind.

His buildings go beyond demonstration of a theory. They are not improvisations. Nor do they display an attitude of complacency with materials and technical devices. He sought to perfect an inner simplicity that at once comprehends mind and feeling, mind and action.

He was fond of saying that a man is greater than his work. If his architecture shows what he achieved, it is also an indication of his potential, of those values which he deeply felt. Through his architecture he communicated those values to his fellow architects.

There are five constants in the work of Louis Kahn: 1) The sense of composition, the integrity of building; 2) Reverence for material; 3) Sense of "room" as the essence of architecture — plan, a society of rooms; 4) Light as maker of structure; 5) Architecture of connection.

1) The Sense of Composition

Kahn's sense of the integrity of building is a meeting point for many of his philosophical considerations. Once while discussing his sense of beauty, Kahn talked about St. Thomas Aquinas' concept of beauty. This was very similar to his own concept of composition. To Aquinas, beauty consisted of four ingredients: 1) Integrity, 2) Wholeness, 3) Symmetry, and 4) Radiance. By integrity he meant that an object is complete and self-sufficient within itself, that it is neither attached to nor dependent upon anything outside it. Looking at a man walking down the street, we know that the body is complete

within itself. It is not a part of the pavement or the sky. By wholeness he meant that all the elements of an object are justifiable, that no part can be taken away without destroying the whole. Symmetry means a balance resulting from the correspondence of parts in a way in which one cannot change without changing the others. Therefore, symmetry is a relationship, a relationship in which each part is totally sympathetic to the others. One knows that each element is well-chosen to respond to the rest. And finally, radiance is a quality that distinguishes it from other objects. It is the "what-ness" that makes it possible to give a name to something: a deer, an owl, a house, etc. It is the integrity with purpose.

It is obvious that St. Thomas Aquinas was thinking about the elements of an entity. His concept of beauty is not an a-priori concept but comes from a reverence for those elements. Kahn's own concept of composition is similar, though his language is often different. For example, his distinction between the "servant" spaces and spaces "to be served" is an indication of his attempt to clarify the character of each of the spatial elements that make up a plan. One of the earliest projects, the Bath House (1, 2, 3) of the Trenton Jewish Community Center, illustrates this distinction clearly. The plan is composed with the four main spaces and their auxiliary elements — the "servant" spaces — each given a definite position. Kahn developed this principle further in the main building of the Community Center (4), where the servant spaces were defined by masonry piers.

But even at the Bath House, not everything was resolved. For example, the entrance to the building had to be indicated by a painted wall (5), since all sides were similar. Kahn once recalled that this was done not

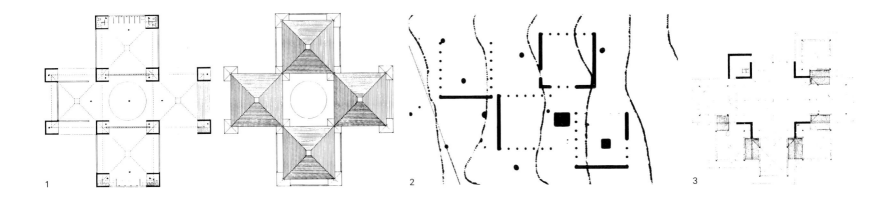

1

2

3

without an awareness that there was still something arbitrary about having to paint a wall to indicate an entrance.

The Adler House (6), which was done at the same time, took the distinction between servant and served spaces one step further. The structure itself is called upon here to make the spatial distinctions. The depth of the stone piers provided the necessary auxiliary spaces around the main living units, thus integrating structure and space. The Richards Laboratory Building at the University of Pennsylvania (7) is the most clear and, at the time of its construction, the most dramatic manifestation of this distinction and integration.

The integration of structure and space was already present at the Yale University Art Gallery (8), which actually preceded the Trenton Bath House. Here the structure itself became the servant space. For this, Kahn invented a system of slab construction, which also carried within itself all the utilities usually housed above a false ceiling, an element Kahn considered unjustifiable. But at Yale, this integration had not been consciously thought out. Kahn became aware of his desire for integration after the

Trenton projects and then, in 1954, he drew a sketch showing the Art Gallery if he were to design it all over again (9).

But even the attempt at such integration at Yale seems somewhat timid compared to its expression at the Salk Institute (10). Here, structure regained its rightful position as more than a mere element of support; it became also a framework of constants, "station points," in the composition of inseparable elements. A hint of this can be seen in the project for the Adath Jeshurun Synagogue (11), where the spatial constants and the structural constants are integrated on the three apexes of the triangular plan (1954).

Structure, as a framework of constants, played an important role in the plan for Philadelphia, Kahn's home town. Once he advised his students at the University of Pennsylvania, who were engaged in a project for Philadelphia, to view the city from such a high vantage point that they see only the two rivers. Kahn's own scheme for the city, done in 1952, was motivated similarly by a desire to build around the city's most fundamental and constant elements. Most of our existing cities have accumulated,

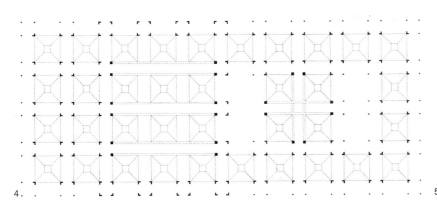

4.

5

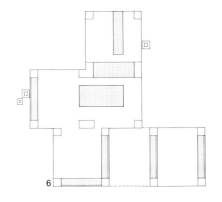

6

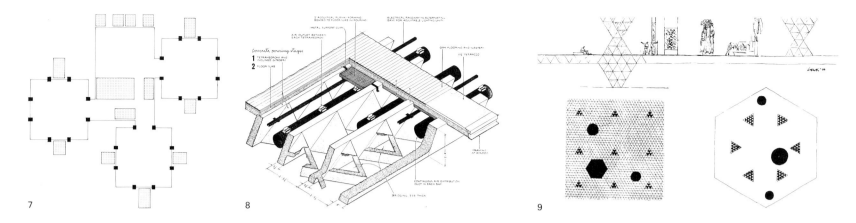

7   8   9

in time, a number of circumstantial decisions which, while valid in themselves, are not always related to each other. The task of an urban designer, then, is to place himself at such a vantage point, both in space and time, that he can envision a moment when cities were still towns, not in terms of their size but in terms of the simplicity and interrelatedness of their elements. Philadelphia, like most other cities, was built before the automobile and was gradually modified with corrective architecture to accommodate the car. In redefining the entire network of roads into a hierarchy of movements, Kahn elevated the dismal and utilitarian aspects of roads and traffic to a poetic composition of movement and communication (12).

The proposal remains unrealized, but the values it articulated will be remembered for a long time.

The plan-composition at Dacca (13) is symbolic in the sense that symbolism is an organ of discovery rather than mere notation. In architecture, as in language, the intangible relations become tangible only when incarnated in symbolic expression. Symbolism, therefore, is concerned with relations much more than the elements of a proposition. The elements themselves are symbolic only in that particular relationship. At Dacca, the plan's significance lies in the relationships expressed through the disposition of its elements. The Citadel of Assembly and the Citadel of the Institutions face each other as if to constantly remind the pragmatic legislative Assembly of the primordial beginnings of human institutions. Also, the arrangement of the Prayer Hall, sitting between the Assembly and the Supreme Court in the original scheme, was a symbolic organization. The very composition suggested not only the relative nature of the activities of Assembly and the Supreme Court — the one dedicated to temporal law and the other to eternal — but also put them in a spiritual context. What better gift can an architect give to a newborn democracy at a time when all around the spiritual perspective of human endeavors is beclouded by pragmatic considerations. Neither the Citadel of the Institution nor the Supreme Court remain where Kahn intended in the beginning. During the lengthy time of construction, the political situation changed dramatically.

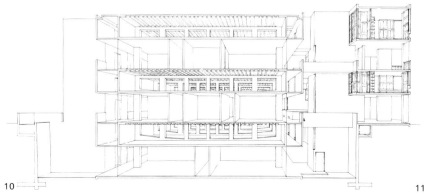

10

11

182

Bangladesh, originally a part of Pakistan, became an independent country, and Dacca, instead of being a provincial capital, became the main administrative as well as symbolic capital of the new country. A new Secretariat is urgently needed now, which will face the assembly complex, and new land has been set aside behind the Secretariat for the Institutions. The Supreme Court has decided to remain in its present quarters.

If the essential elements of composition were present from the beginning at Dacca, Kahn had to go through a long and painstaking search for them at Fort Wayne Fine Arts Center (14). In the process, the elements themselves changed. Some were entirely dropped and a few new ones added. However, there was something arbitrary about this. What was lacking from the beginning was something that would take away the arbitrariness in it. The Court, which Kahn referred to as the "Court of the Entrances," (15) became this element. The restlessness

of the earlier schemes is gone; there is a quietness about the latest scheme as if the radiance of which Thomas Aquinas spoke is realized.

Unfortunately, at Fort Wayne, as at Dacca, Kahn could not realize his vision in its entirety. Only the Theater of Performing Arts is built, and even there many of the elements that Kahn wanted — such as a chapel for the actors, and a place "for the actors to be alone with their soliloquy" — could not be realized. However, Kahn said that what is not built is not really lost. Once their value is established, their demand for presence is undeniable. They are just waiting for the right circumstances. Only a few months before his death, Kahn was asked to participate, with Kenzo Tange, in designing the new institutional and commercial center for Tehran. His first sketch shows all those elements and considerations which were originally present at Dacca but were later given up. In fact, this situation points toward the very prerogative as

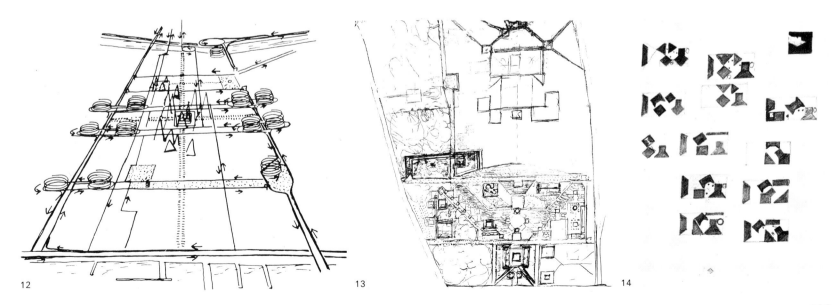

12 13 14

well as limitation of a profession which must, by necessity, take into consideration factors and circumstances which are not always controlled by the architect. The very acceptance of these circumstances and a determination to try again and again make it all very human.

There is a historical aspect to Kahn's concern for composition. Composition of elements was a preoccupation of the Beaux-Arts academic tradition at the turn of the century. Julien Guadet, the respected professor at the Ecole des Beaux-Arts, wrote about it, and his famous pupil, Tony Garnier, may have set in motion forces and attitudes which, no matter how well disguised by subsequent events in architecture, may still be with us. This may explain the association which Kahn is supposed to have with the Beaux-Arts academic tradition. However, it was Auguste Choisy, a contemporary as well as an ideological antagonist of Guadet, who influenced Kahn more — not by his words and ideas (Kahn did not read French and was not a "reader" in the scholarly sense) but by the magnificent illustrations in his book *Histoire de l'Architecture* (16, 17), which Kahn treasured (18). Choisy's main thesis might have been Universalist in that he believed technique and construction to be the raison d'être for form, but nothing could illustrate the most essential compositional elements of a building more clearly than his highly stylized illustrations. His words may have reinforced three generations of rationalist architecture, but, not having access to his words, Kahn "read" into his book an attitude that remained unverbalized. Thus, it is possible that Kahn succeeded in bridging the gap between the French academic and classical tradition on one side and 20th century rationalism on the other by defining a general frame of reference — order —

within which both the aesthetic and the technical aspects of architecture could find validity.

2) Reverence for Material

The second constant in Kahn's work, his reverence for material, is also rooted in the academic tradition of pre-industrial time — a reverence born out of a direct, one-to-one relationship between man and the material unit of his construction — stone. The awareness of this relationship in earlier times led man to an awe and respect for nature, the source of this material, and for her laws, which guided its use. With increasing industrialization and as the materials began to be manufactured, this relationship between man and material became more and more obscure. The disparity between the process of making the material and the process of construction is one of the saddest facts of contemporary architecture. The re-

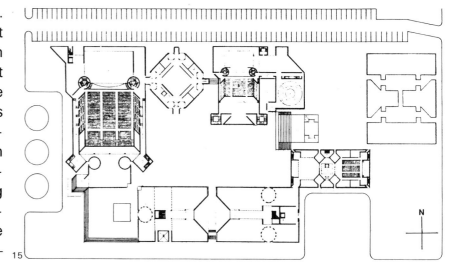

15

sultant forms are unsatisfactory, since they are usually forms of the past transposed on new materials. Kahn's buildings, however, stand out as uncompromising integration of matter, form, and process. The purpose is not so much to experiment with new material for its own sake, but to re-establish the relationship between man and nature through a diligent use of her materials. In his buildings, Kahn followed the dictates of the materials themselves, as if they were alive and talking to him. In doing so, he revealed hitherto undiscovered potentials of those materials. He never concealed his materials beneath other materials. The concrete walls at the Salk Institute are a careful expression of the technology of concrete; and the Richards Laboratory is perhaps the first truly precast concrete building, where even the crane itself was an element of composition from the beginning. (Another project in which the crane plays an important role is the Roosevelt Memorial in New York, soon to be built. It is made of units of granite 6' × 6' × 12', determined by the maximum weight a crane can carry.)

His work in India and Bangladesh brought him the opportunity to use brick, not only the most commonly used material there but also the most practical. In the hands of Kahn, this traditional material has suddenly come alive as if it were a brand new material. It is blended with concrete in a true compositional sense, exploiting new potentials of brick as well as strengthening its weaknesses with concrete (19). Kahn seemed to challenge nature to provide him with the instruments of expression, but, at the same time, followed the dictates of her laws with the utmost humility. Material, for Kahn, was not an antagonist to be commanded to obedience, but a friendly partner, almost anthropomorphic.

The lessons learned at Dacca and Ahmedabad in the use of brick and concrete together found different expressions in the Library at Philip Exeter Academy (20), in the

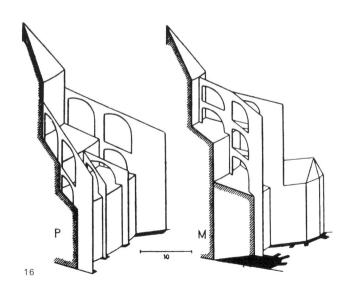

16

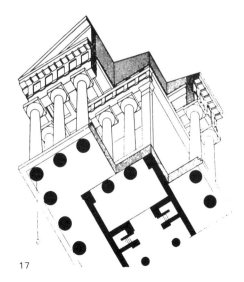

17

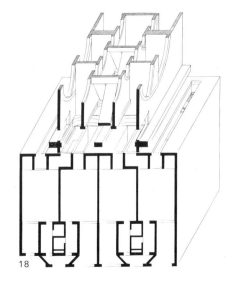

18

Theater in Fort Wayne (21), and later in the Hurva Synagogue in Jerusalem (22). All these buildings are composed of two distinct "zones," one wrapping around the other. The inner zone, requiring large span with greater load-carrying capacity, is given to concrete, while the outer zone, made of brick (or stone at Hurva), contains activities requiring small intimate spaces, which also protect the inside from the elements. Here again, we see evidence of a blend of the classical attitude (as opposed to classical form) and a formal language based upon the rational use of material and technique, which Choisy would have approved.

3) Sense of "Room" as Essence of Architecture — Plan, a Society of Rooms

When Kahn said that a plan is a society of rooms, he was talking about composition of spatial elements. However, his concept of "Room" deserves special attention (23). If the plan is a composition of spatial elements, "Room" is its unit, often with an existence independent of the plan form. But for Kahn, this unit is not an abstract entity, such as implied by "space" in contemporary architecture,

19

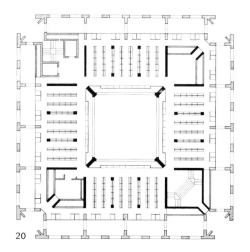

20

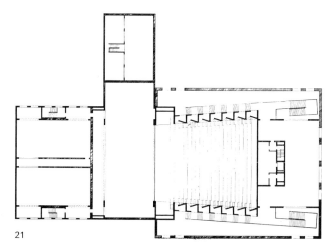

21

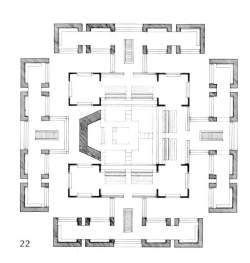

22

Architecture comes from The Making of a Room
The Plan A society of rooms is a place good to live work learn

The Room

A great American Poet once asked The Architect "What slice of the sun does your building have, what light enters your Room as if to say the sun never knew how great it is until it struck the side of a building.

s The place of the mind. In a small room one does not say what one would in a large room. In a room with only one other person could be generative. The vectors of each meet. A room is not a room without natural light. Natural light gives the time of day and the mood of the seasons to enter.

23

but concrete, corporeal and, above all, human. Here Kahn was working with a keen perception of the human activities: their rhythm, their light, and the subtle transition between different activities. Defining in such simple terms the identity of architectural space is one of the basic contributions of Louis Kahn. For Kahn, a room where two persons can communicate was fundamentally different from one where there is a gathering of many. "The difference is simply that of one being an event and the other a performance." Few architects have recognized the subtle link between place and activity. A plan, then, is a recognition of the very rhythm of life. In this, Kahn rejects the plastic continuity of space as an expression of the multiplicity of life in favor of the identity and

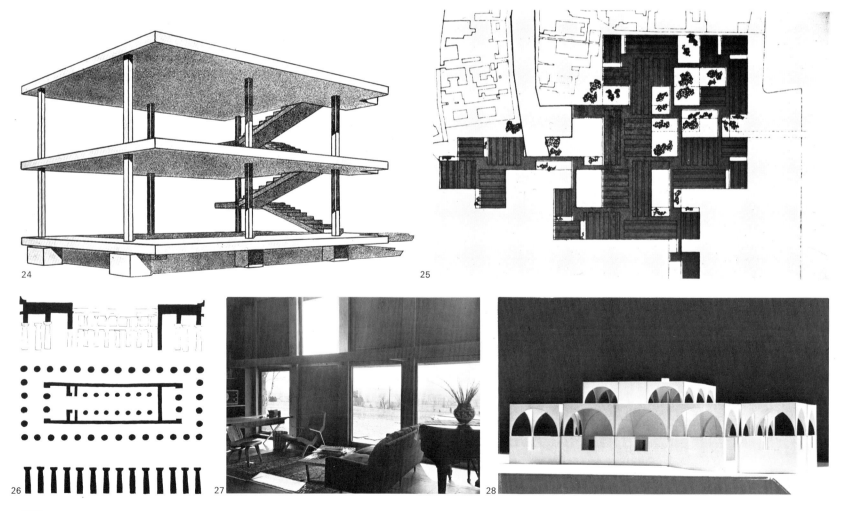

24

25

26

27

28

appropriateness of each of the spatial elements. This is not easy since it requires an integration between structural and spatial units, a factor rejected by modern architecture since Le Corbusier's declaration in 1915 of a functional independence between skeleton and wall (24). However, what Corbusier was declaring was a discovery of a possibility inherent in the new technology. He, himself, never lost sight of the discipline that called for the integration of all the elements into one unified whole (25).

4) Light as Maker of Structure

For Kahn, though, this integration meant a redefinition of structure itself, which brings us to the fourth constant in his work: light as the maker of structure. Natural light determines the identity of a room. The plan indicates where the light is and where it is not. He made a sketch of the Parthenon to illustrate this point (26). It shows a plan and a section with only the elements that obstruct light drawn in black. These elements — the walls and the columns — are also the structural elements of the building. There is nothing that is not needed.

This natural economy of elements has been a preoccupation of Kahn from the beginning, though not always so clearly expressed. In the early projects it comes through as a desire to understand and establish a rationale for an opening in the wall. Puncturing a hole in the wall to make a window must have seemed quite arbitrary to him. Thus, at the Weiss House (27), the walls are made with vertically movable panels that change positions, depending upon the need for light. At the Fleisher House (28) and later at the "Tribune Review" building (29), the shape of the opening itself was determined by light. To this another element was added at the Luanda Consulate (30), a free-standing wall with an opening in front of the window wall, thereby controlling both the sunlight and the glare. One of the most unusual expressions of this is the series of cylinders of light at the Mikveh Israel Synagogue in Philadelphia (31). There, light is given a volumetric form as opposed to a two dimensional window. In all these buildings, though, a conscious connection

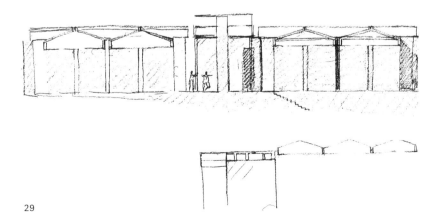

29

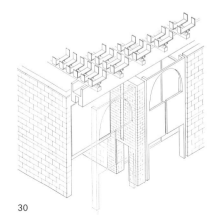

30

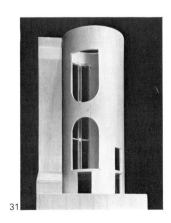

31

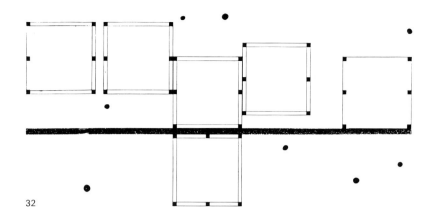

32

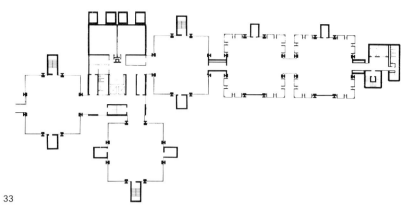

33

between light and structure is not evident. But parallel to this search for the architecture of light was another approach, which was to become much more significant later. Starting with the Yale Art Gallery, Kahn seems to be looking for maximum economy in composition. He envisioned structure as a series of spatial units, their support elements also determining the openings between, which became either light or servant spaces. The two residences designed in 1955, the Adler House (6) and the DeVore House (32), as well as the Trenton Jewish Community Center designed in the same year (unfortunately none of these came to be built), helped evolve a discipline which, a few years later, integrated all previous concerns into one single edifice: the Richards Medical Research Building (33). The plan of the building is structured with a series of "studio" units, 48' square, with columns on the third point. The openings between the columns are given either to light or to service towers or to connection between other units.

In one of his more recent projects, the rebuilding of a city block in Houston, Kahn devised a "plan-form" with a series of "rooms" whose identification with activities is determined by the intensity of their structures. One does not have to name a room; it earns its own — which may

even change in time by its power of suggestion, the determining factor being its light. Structure is thus again defined as an element of organization of human activities, of places in which it is good to learn, to meet, to express, to be. In rejecting the independence between skeleton and wall, between spatial and structural units, Kahn has made the technological events architectural. If Corbusier's proclamation stemmed from his recognition of the freedom offered by new technology, Kahn discovered the freedom inherent in architecture. What was at Trenton still somewhat rigid and self-conscious has gained a certain freedom at Houston.

5) Architecture of Connection

"Architecture of connection" is an obvious extension of composition. The problem of connecting the various elements of composition, both physically as well as symbolically, has been a preoccupation of architecture throughout history. The approaches have been either axial (34), picturesque (35), or geometrical, such as at Isfahan (36) or with the introduction of special connecting elements, such as in Hadrian's Villa (37) and in Corbusier's La Tourette (38). In all these, though the instruments

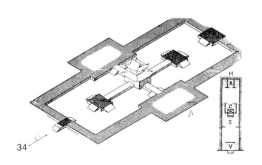

34

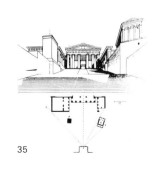

35

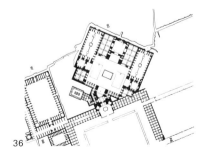

36

37

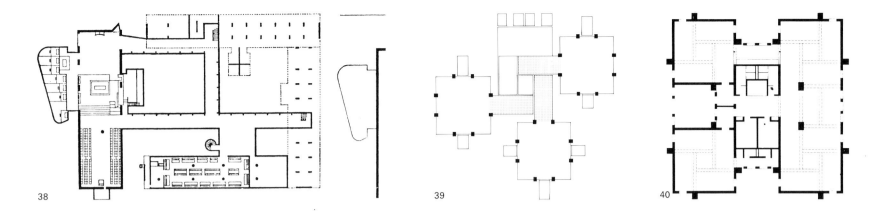

38   39   40

have differed, the concern has always been compositional. It is natural, therefore, that Kahn, too, realized the need to define connection as an element of composition.

Here again, structure generates connection. The arbitrariness of making an opening to connect one room with the other, or the use of an additional element, such as a corridor, is avoided by organizing the structure itself in such a way that the opening between two supporting elements automatically provides connection. Thus, at both the Adler House and the DeVore House, rooms are shifted slightly out of axis so that obvious places for doors are "found." This almost naïve and still somewhat arbitrary method was later developed into a centrifugal arrangement at the Richards Medical Towers (39) and the Mill Creek Community building (40).

But it was at Bryn Mawr that the problem of connection was tackled with imagination. The three squares with their corners overlapping allowed Kahn the most obvious

and inevitable location for entry (41). The plan has both an economy and an intensity that come from the obviousness of this decision.

If the rigid, geometrical configuration of the dormitory building seems static, this certainly is not the case at the Fisher House or at the project for the Congregation of Dominican Sisters (42). In both these buildings, the programmatic elements are clearly articulated. As a result, each of the elements has an independent structural integrity that is appropriate. Kahn has taken full advantage of this freedom.

The above survey of the common denominators in Kahn's architecture suggests that his work has been guided by concerns which have always been present in the practice of architecture. His work is "non-historical" in the sense that we use the word "timeless." We prefer "non-historical" to draw attention to the point that it is neither a "linear" extension of the primary attitudes that have dominated modern architecture nor a simple,

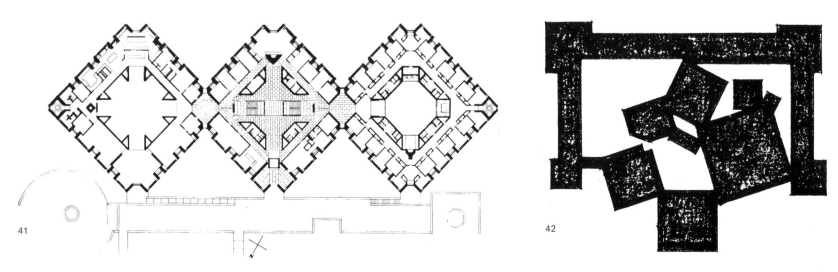

41   42

rational resolution of past debates. This point has been expanded upon in other parts of this book. But suffice it to say here that these timeless aspects of architecture, which are often forgotten in the heat of ideological debates, do not necessarily have to be at odds with the urgency of the moment.

We have, where necessary, drawn examples from the past, both distant and near, with the hope of conveying the sense that, while instruments and emphasis change in time, there are fundamental qualities of architecture which are essentially non-historical. As Kahn said, "Boullée is, therefore Architecture is (43)."

43

The Place of Work

1 A.N. Richards Medical Research
  Laboratory and University of
  Pennsylvania
  Biological Research Laboratory
  Philadelphia, Pennsylvania

2 "Tribune Review" Building
  Greensburg, Pennsylvania

3 U.S. Consulate
  Luanda, Angola

4 Olivetti-Underwood Plant
  Harrisburg, Pennsylvania

5 Kansas City Office Tower
  Kansas City, Kansas

The Place of Work

Five projects presented on the same scale.

1 A. N. Richards Medical Research Laboratory and University of Pennsylvania Biological Research Laboratory, Philadelphia, Pennsylvania.
2 "Tribune Review" Building, Greensburg, Pennsylvania.
3 U.S. Consulate, Luanda, Angola.
4 Kansas City Office Tower, Kansas City, Kansas.
5 Olivetti-Underwood Plant, Harrisburg, Pennsylvania.

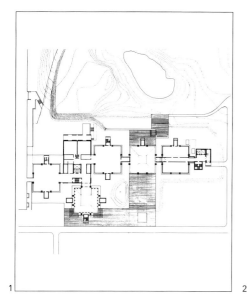

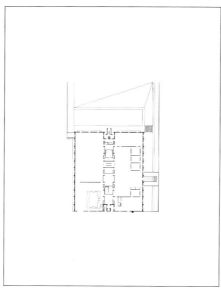

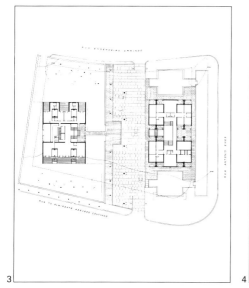

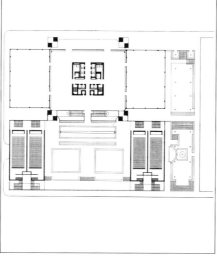

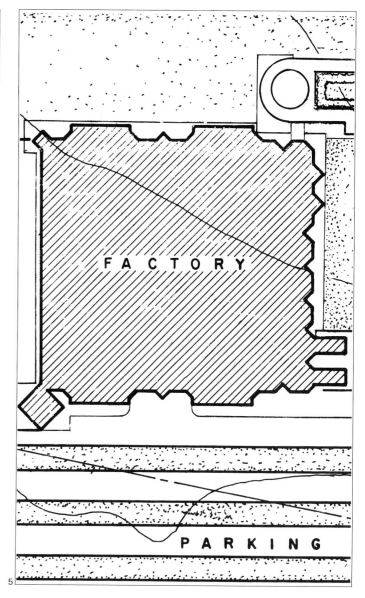

FACTORY

PARKING

1 A.N. Richards Medical Research Laboratory and University of Pennsylvania
Biological Research Laboratory
Philadelphia, Pennsylvania

1957–1961
Structural Engineer: August Komendant

Several elements of Kahn's architecture came together in this building, elements that were used before, independently of each other: a clear articulation of servant and served spaces; the problem of light; the integration of spatial, structural, and utility elements; and, above all, the integration of form, material, and process. As a result, this building represents a significant turning point in contemporary architecture.

The intense intellectual rigor employed in the building is manifested in the several stages the plan went through and in every detail of the building. The building was designed in two phases: the medical laboratories, which form a cluster of three towers around a central complex, preceded the biological laboratories which join them.

View looking east.

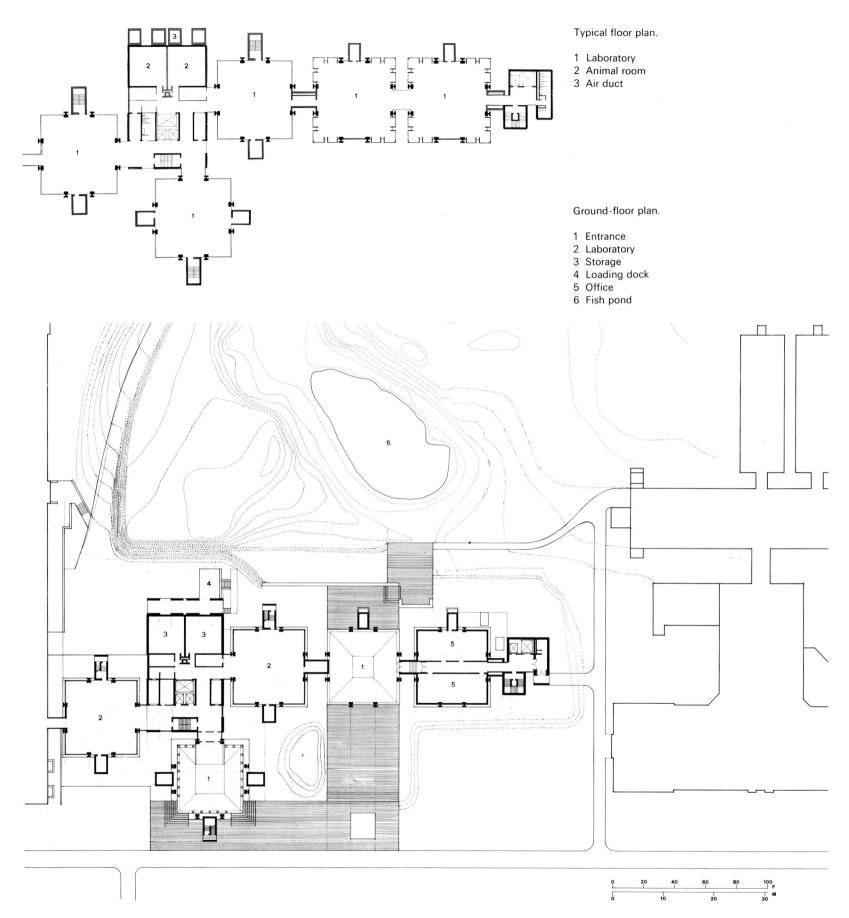

Typical floor plan.

1 Laboratory
2 Animal room
3 Air duct

Ground-floor plan.

1 Entrance
2 Laboratory
3 Storage
4 Loading dock
5 Office
6 Fish pond

The core in the medical laboratory is a poured-in-place utility tower with slabs supported by load-bearing walls, which enclose elevators, stairs, lavatories, animal quarters, etc. These facilities are shared by three eight-story towers which surround it. Each of these towers is, in turn, flanked by sub-towers, which contain exit stairs, exhaust stacks, and piping.

All vertical circulation of services and people is thus confined to the periphery, leaving each laboratory floor free of any interruptions. The columns are located at the periphery, forming a triangle, leaving the corners open.

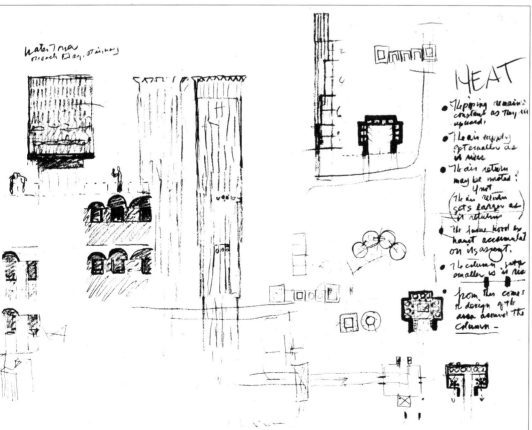

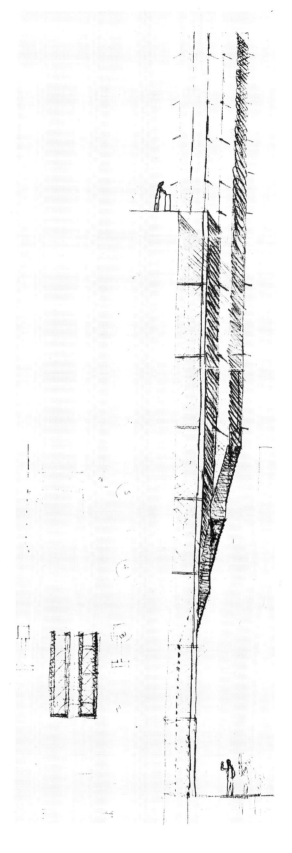

The Service towers – Study sketches and notes on various versions.

View looking south — before the Biology building was constructed.

View looking west.

The integration of architecture and construction is achieved through a structural system consisting of four basic prefabricated concrete units, each interlocking with the others. Each studio tower is a self-contained structural unit. The building remains a record of how it is put together.

The biology building is essentially an extension of the same discipline, though the structure is simplified and the problem of glare in the working area is solved differently. An added element is the study carrels on the two upper floors. The primary materials are concrete, brick, and glass.

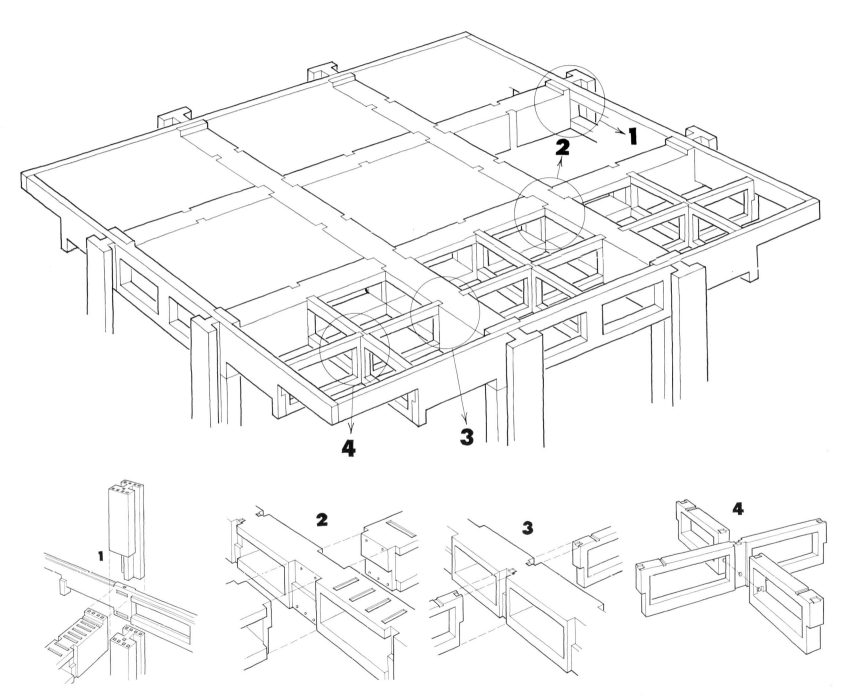

Construction with the four basic units. ▷

The high-rise closed structures are service shafts for the installations, which increase in number on the upper floors.

2 "Tribune Review" Building
Greensburg, Pennsylvania

1958–1961

The building serves as both offices and printing plant for a small local newspaper.

Construction consists of load-bearing brick piers with in-fill walls of concrete masonry units and precast planks for roof slab.

The interior is lit by a system of windows which allow natural light to fill the rooms without causing glare.

1 Public entrance
2 Offices
3 Editor
4 Advertising and Business Managers
5 Mail room
6 News room
7 Composing room
8 Stereotype department
9 Press room
10 Service (mezzanine above)
11 Mailboy's room

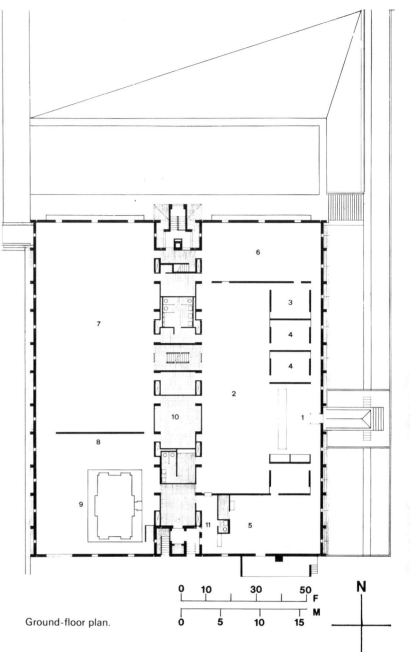

Ground-floor plan.

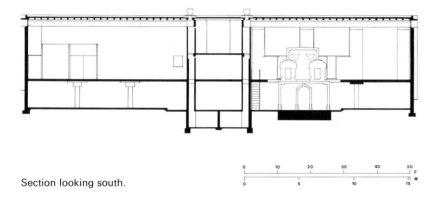

Section looking south.

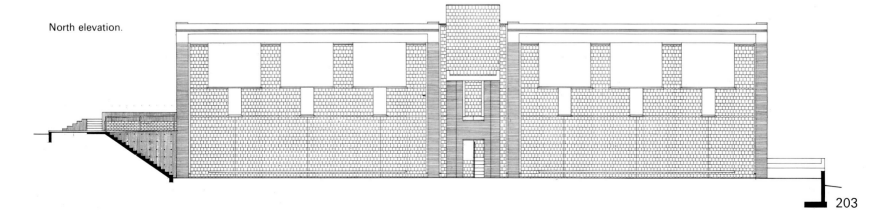

North elevation.

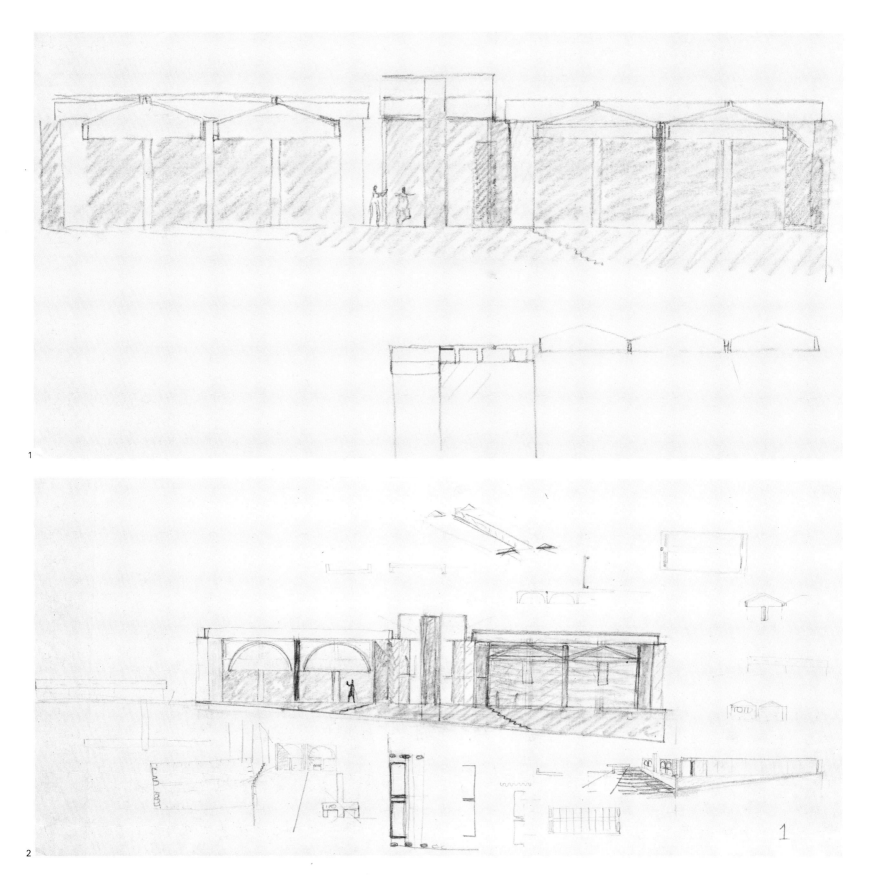

1/2 Elevation studies. Note the variations on the design of windows.
3 The north façade.
4 The News room.
5 Detail of south façade.

3

4

5

3 U.S. Consulate
Luanda, Angola

Project 1959–1961

The project consists of two buildings: the Chancellery and the Consul's Residence.

Both buildings are distinguished by a unique solution to the problem of hot sun and glaring light.

Free-standing walls, with large openings standing in front of the windows, modify the light and reduce the glare, while the roof consists of an independent "sun roof" of precast concrete elements 6 feet above the normal slab, thus minimizing the sun's impact.

Construction is of precast concrete and concrete masonry units.

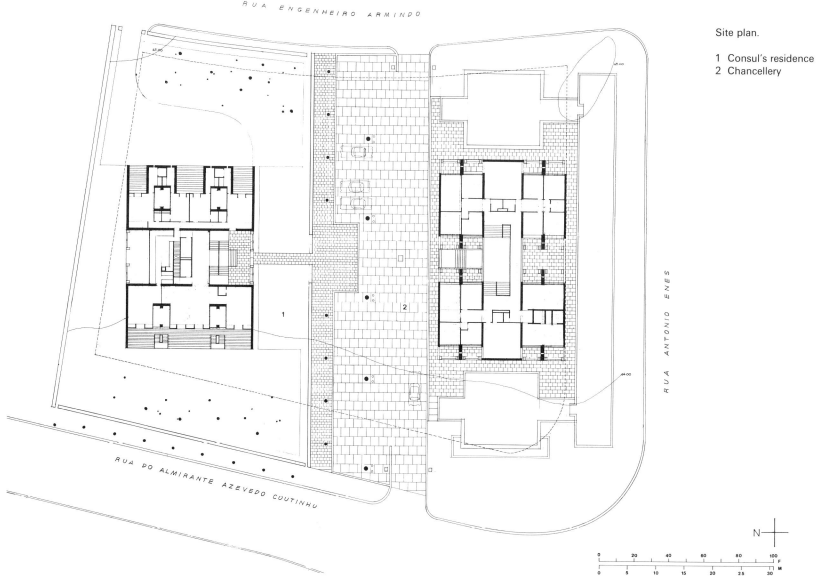

Site plan.

1 Consul's residence
2 Chancellery

Northeast elevation view. The residence building and the consulate are both severely symmetrical. The parasol roof of heat-reflecting tiles is totally separated from the continuous waterproof roof beneath it (cf. detail, p. 209, fig. 4). The unbearable solar radiation of these regions is mitigated by perforated walls, whose semicircular apertures and slits require no glass.

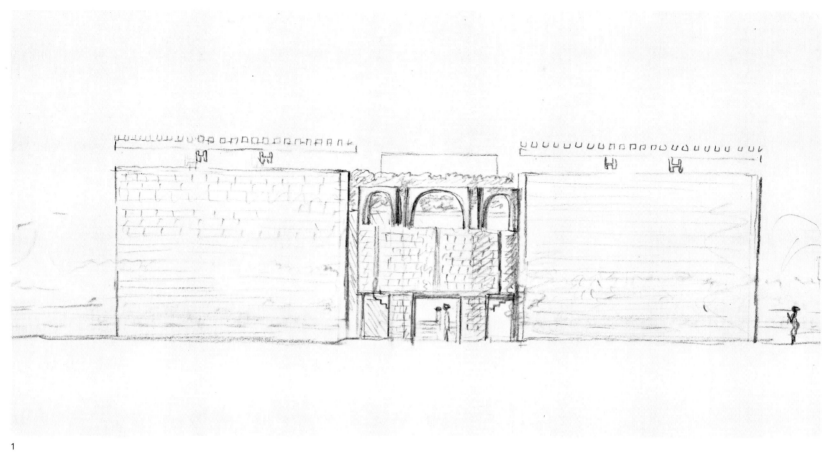

1

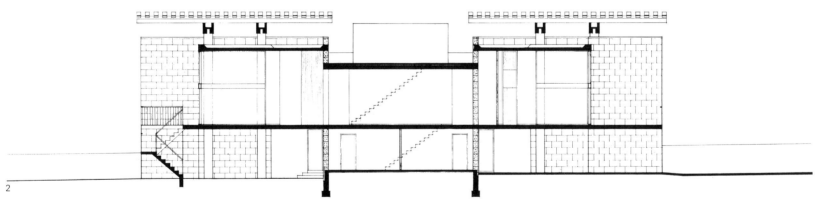

2

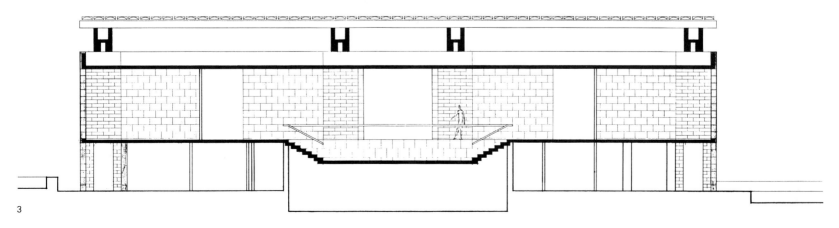

3

208

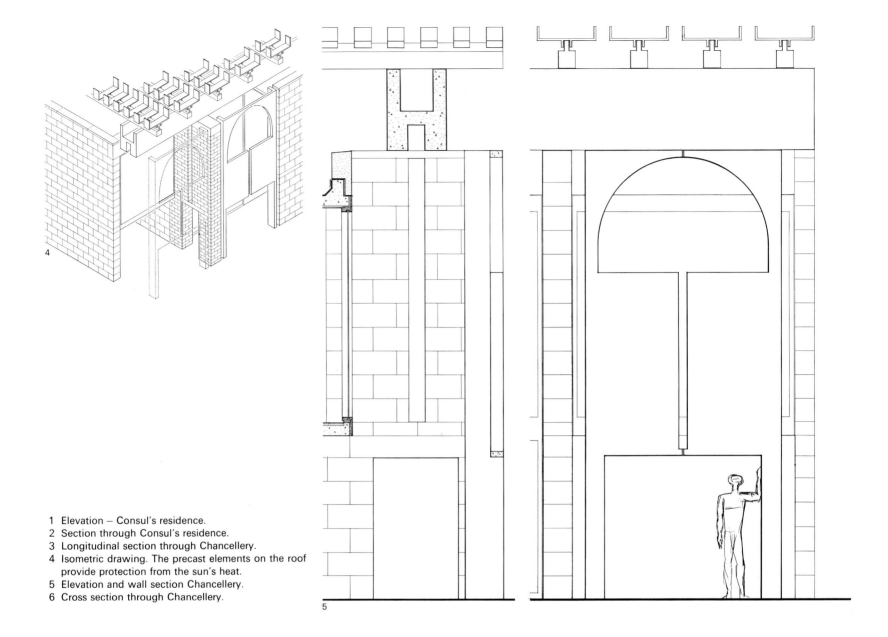

1 Elevation – Consul's residence.
2 Section through Consul's residence.
3 Longitudinal section through Chancellery.
4 Isometric drawing. The precast elements on the roof
  provide protection from the sun's heat.
5 Elevation and wall section Chancellery.
6 Cross section through Chancellery.

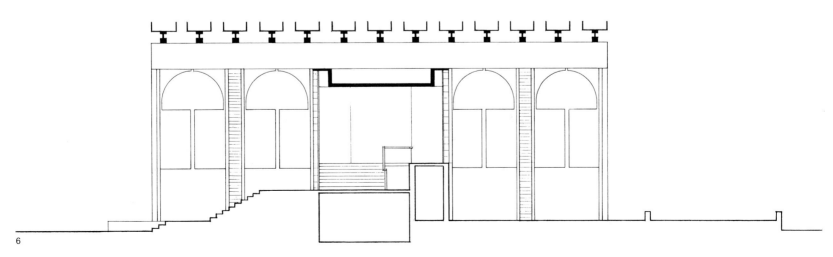

4 Olivetti-Underwood Plant
Harrisburg, Pennsylvania

1966–1970

Site plan. The lower part of the terrain is for parking.

Concrete umbrellas, 60 feet apart, make up the main working area. The hexagonally-shaped umbrellas are joined together in a way which makes possible openings for natural light throughout the work space. These openings are covered with specially designed fiberglass skylights.

Administrative spaces and the cafeteria are located on one side of the work space. The height of the umbrellas makes it possible to introduce a mezzanine floor for offices, where large heights are not required.

The utilities are exposed and integrated with the structural elements. The exterior wall is made of cinder blocks left in their natural state.

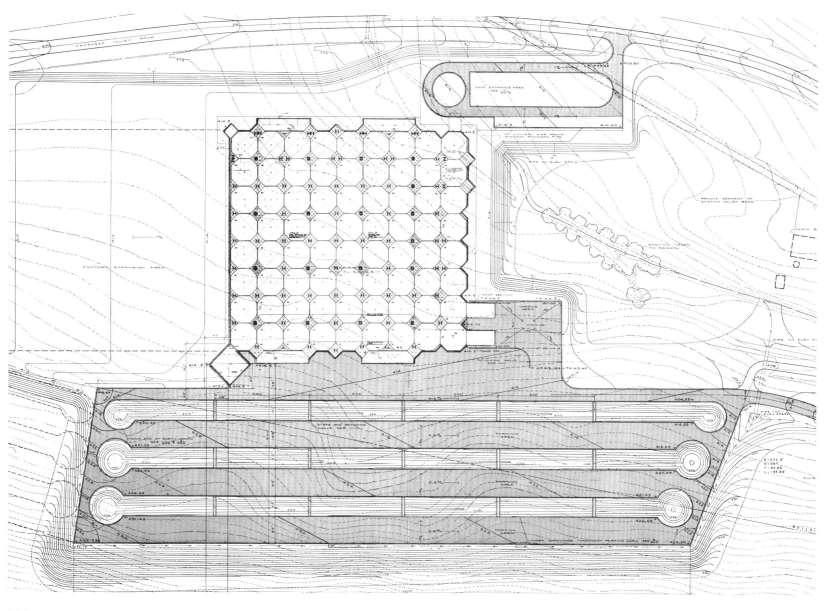

1 View looking east.
2 Interior of the factory.
3 Detail – The fiberglass skylight.

5 Kansas City Office Tower
Kansas City, Kansas

1966–1973
Structural Engineer: August Komendant

A speculative office building must be constructed in the shortest possible time. From the beginning, Kahn included the process of construction as a consideration in design. The utility core and the four corners of the tower are to be built first, with a continuously moving formwork. The columns on the corners support trusses from which floors will be suspended. The trusses enclose a two-level clubhouse, and the podium contains places to meet and shop.

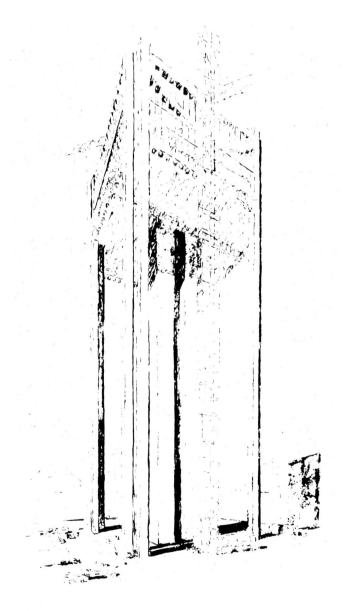

Perspective drawing of tower under construction.

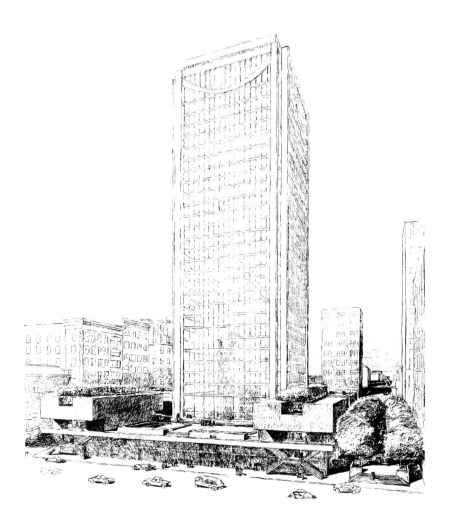

Perspective view.

Parterre level.

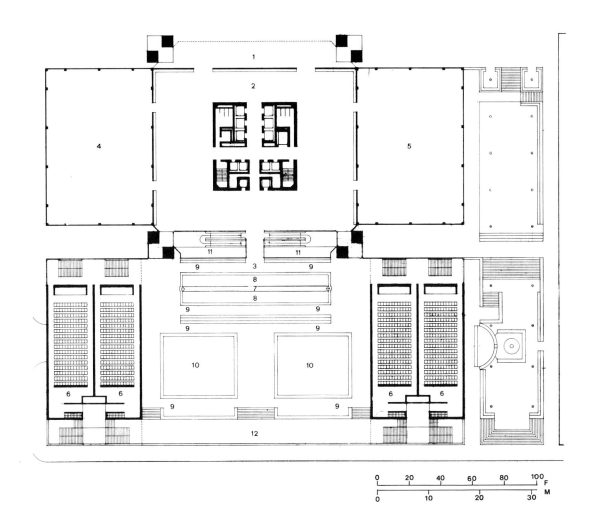

1 Baltimore Street entrance
2 Lobby
3 Parterre entrance
4 Bank
5 Brokerage
6 Theater
7 Fountain
8 Pool
9 Seating
10 Garden
11 Light well
12 Terrace

Plan for floors 18.   Plan for club floor 29.

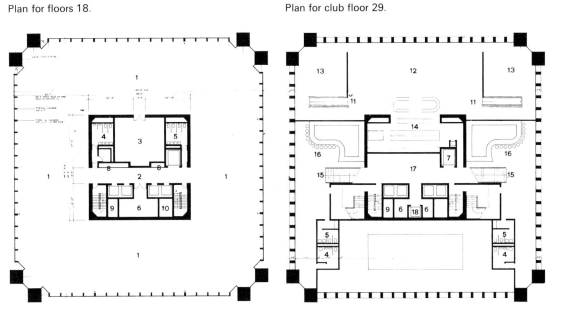

1 Office space
2 Core
3 Library/conference room
4 Men's toilet
5 Women's toilet
6 Mechanical room
7 Freight elevator
8 Electrical closet
9 Exhaust air shaft
10 Fresh air shaft
11 Stairs down to club lounge
12 Club dining-room
13 Sitting-room
14 Kitchen
15 Stairs up to dining
16 Bar
17 Service area
18 Service elevator

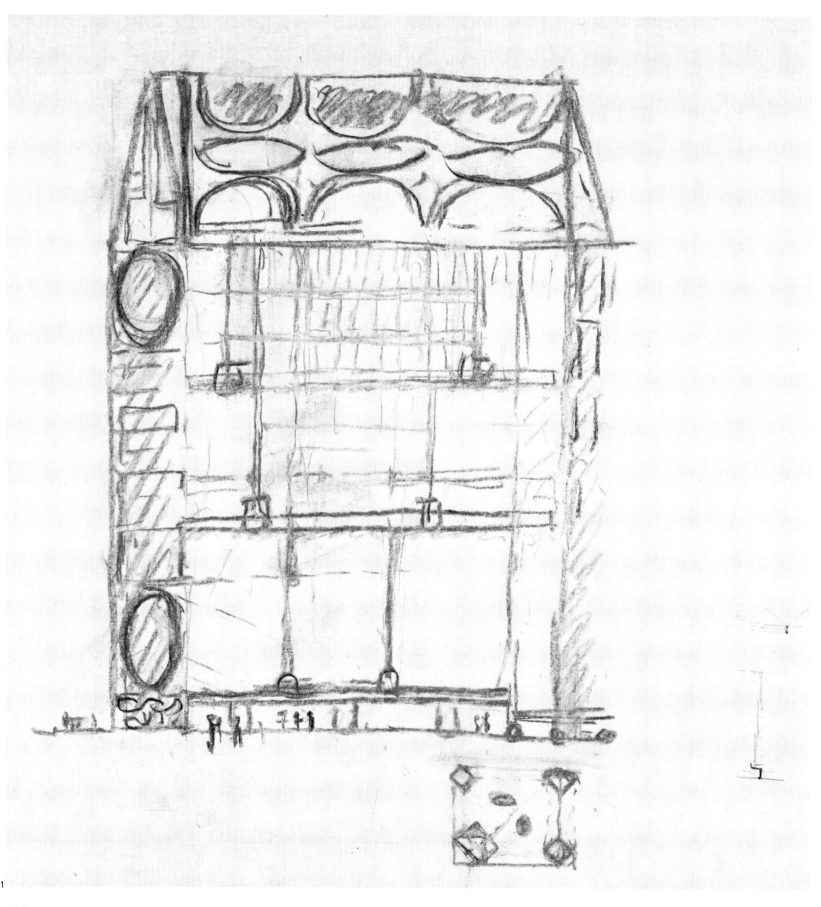

1 One of the first study sketches of the tower building.
   Note the floors are suspended from above.
2 Building section.
3 Model of Office tower.

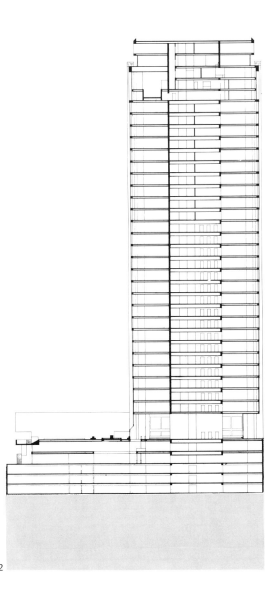

2

3

The Universal and the Eternal

The architecture of Louis Kahn has brought into sharp focus an attitude that raises fundamental questions regarding the nature and purpose of architecture itself. This attitude is neither an extension nor a resolution of the debate on the nature of architecture, which has engaged us for the first half of the century. Rather, it is rooted in one man's intense desire to transcend time. Obviously, Louis Kahn is not an isolated event outside the mainstream of modern architecture. His buildings are accepted as examples of modern architecture. But we do not have the proper theoretical and historical perspective with which to view his thought and work. It is the purpose of this chapter to offer such a perspective.

Even though the theoretical manifestations of modern architecture have taken many forms, there is one powerful attitude that seems to permeate all — an attitude that holds "reason" as a supreme human value. Though rationalism itself, as a philosophical schema, has been in existence since the 17th century, it was not until the end of the last century that it began to penetrate architectural thinking. Within a generation, it had not only taken hold of the entire spectrum of architectural activity, but also, in large measure, modified the very nature of that activity.

The work of Louis Kahn is guiding a shift of emphasis, a change of locus, away from rationalism. Therefore, it is important at this point to see his work in the context of rationalism. We have tried to do this by briefly articulating the main features of rationalism in architecture and viewing the emphasis in Kahn's thought against this background. It is not our intention either to evaluate one in terms of the other, or to compare the two attitudes.

There have been a number of parallel, and occasionally contradictory, developments in architecture in this century. One can list these as 1) Universalism, 2) Civic Accountability, 3) Unification of Visual Arts, and 4) Integration of Industrial Vocabulary. All of these developments seem rooted in rationalism.

1) Universalism

Universalism began in the desire among architects to legitimatize their work in relation to other, more "objective" activities of man, such as technology. For this, architecture has to be founded on the most objective and universally acceptable attributes of man. Reason is held to be such a universal attribute of the human species. While the concept of reality may be a product of cultural variables, the basic patterns of thinking are believed to be common to all civilizations. It is the awareness of this universalism that is at the heart of Auguste Choisy's interpretation of architecture in his *Histoire de l'Architecture* which appeared in 1899 and exercised tremendous influence on two generations of architects. Choisy's theme was that expressive form was only a logical result of technique, and that it undergoes similar choices and follows similar laws with every people.

Choisy's thesis was well-received by the next generation of European architects. The two prominent European movements, "Bauhaus" and "De Stijl," were universalist in essence, though their interpretations differed.

Bauhaus began with a belief in an objective approach coupled with a vigorous use of reason in its pursuit of a more "humane" architecture. The search for an aesthetic authenticity led to an intellectual discipline until then unknown to architecture. Standardization was introduced and accepted in an attempt to establish a relationship among matter, form, and process. It was this discipline which led Oskar Schlemmer to write for the first Bauhaus Exhibition in 1923:

"Reason and science, 'man's greatest powers,' are the regents, and the engineer is the sedate executor of unlimited possibilities. Mathematics, structure, and mechanization are the elements, and power and money are the dictators of this modern phenomena of steel, concrete, glass, and electricity. Velocity of rigid matter, dematerialization of matter, organization of inorganic matter: all these produce the miracle of abstraction. Based on the laws of nature, these are the achievements of mind in the conquest of nature."

De Stijl, unlike Bauhaus, never abdicated the responsibility for stylistic resolution. Though both groups represented space on the principle of its divisibility and relativity, the sense data — the raw information — remained the link between the image and reality. Both the Rietveld chair and the Mies chair had universalist aspirations. The differences and contradictions were not those of attitude but of style.

Universalism was not limited to Europe alone. In fact, it was at the very foundation of American society. The clarity and simplicity with which a causal relationship was established between form and function, between image and purpose, was typically American. It was also typical of America to proclaim an "International Style," for the architecture that resulted after the transplantation of Bauhaus and De Stijl in the United States was to be based on reason and objectivity, the universal attributes of man.

2) Civic Accountability

Civic accountability is a natural ally of universalism. The universality of reason implies an essential equality among men. It is not surprising, therefore, for reason itself to become an emotional issue among the middle class — though the meaning and application of reason has changed with the changing needs of the time. It was used against the church by science and philosophy and for social change by the Marxists.

The implications of holding reason as the supreme value are threefold. First, nature and society are viewed in a deterministic way, as rational systems essentially determined in their evolution by natural laws. Second, nature and society are comprehensible by human reason and, therefore, changeable by purposeful actions of man — meaning that man's relationship with society and nature is essentially that of control. Third, rationalism patterns not only social life but the individual as well on the model of nature, subject to the law of predictability. Society is seen from the point of view of social contacts and variously formulated patterns of associations. It is precisely for this reason that rationalism has never been able to escape worshipping the utilitarian values of efficiency and rational productive organization.

Architectural thinking had to be revised and modified in order for it to participate meaningfully in the new social and economic outlook of the late 19th and early 20th centuries; this was done in two ways:

On the one hand, all acts of man were seen as meaningful only to the extent that they exercised man's prerogative to control and change social reality, which was seen to be oppressive. Architecture was judged for its commitment to equality for all men. Architectural vocabulary was vigorously purged of all elements seeking to express anything but utilitarian and functional values. Inherent in this approach was the danger of changing the nature of architectural activity into something other than art. This danger was met by reevaluating the nature of art itself. Commenting on the "De Stijl" Manifesto V, Van Doesburg and Van Eesteren wrote in 1923:

"We have to realize that art and life are no longer separate domains. Therefore, the idea of 'art' as illusion unconnected with real life has to disappear. The word 'art' no longer means anything to us. Leaving this concept behind us, we demand the construction of our environment according to creative laws derived from a fixed principle. These laws, linked with those of economics, mathematics, technology, hygiene, etc. lead to new plastic unity."

On the other hand, the rationality of the thinking man as the ultimate basis of a rational organization of society was interpreted to mean that man, the creator of universal concepts, was necessarily free; this freedom, in turn, was interpreted as providing the basis for subjectivity. This approach, unlike the first, refused the criteria of social commitment and civic accountability of architecture and sought to reaffirm the expressive nature of art. Piet Mondrian wrote in "De Stijl" journal under the heading "The Rationality of Neo-Plasticism":

"The man of truly modern culture lives in concrete reality, which his mind transforms into abstractions; his real life moves into the abstract — but, in turn, he makes the abstract real."

The ability of this approach to accept the new social reality was dependent upon its ability to transform and conceptualize that reality. This was done much later — after the period of the International Congresses of Modern Architecture (CIAM) — when the principles of "change" and "growth" of social organizations were articulated and transformed into spatial organization.

Urbanism was a logical step in the direction of expanding the scope and scale of architectural activity to make it more accountable to changing social realities. In fact, cities began to demand architects' attention more and more as it became apparent that a reciprocal relationship existed between the institutional structure of a society and its built environment. However, in the true fashion of rationalism, the new city was viewed as a neatly packaged system of functions. The 'Athens Charter' of CIAM lists these functions as housing, work, recreation and traffic.

3) Unification of Visual Arts

The unification of all the visual arts under a single vocabulary of primary categories was an inevitable response to the new technological and socio-economic conditions. It was felt that in order to meet the new demands, the very nature and purpose of art would have to be revised; this required a radical change in language from figurative to abstract and non-figurative.

The idea that the visible world becomes a real world only through the operation of thought implies that reality is comprised only of those categories in which thought is capable of comprehending, and which can be subjected to rational analysis. These were assumed to be the primary Newtonian categories of space, time, mass, and motion. It was obvious that the iconographic and symbolic aspects of art were sacrificed in favor of the pure plastic vocabulary of planes, lines, right angles, and primary colors — making the differences between the visual arts almost nonexistent.

Ironically this new design consciousness, made possible en masse by industrial production methods, created a good-mannered middle class who demanded an equally good-mannered architecture. This may have been one of the built-in conflicts of rationalism, for the new clientele effectively resisted attempts to make architecture more responsive to social conditions. The new aesthetic demands made the link between image and purpose passive.

4) Integration of Industrial Vocabulary

Logic came to be consciously viewed not only as an element of control but as an element in its own right in organizing the image. Corbusier wrote of a "mathematical lyricism" as being superior to mere sense perception. Inevitably, machine and the products of machine emerged as epitomes of this new lyricism.

The problem of the renewal of architecture to correspond to the new lyricism was thought to be simply a problem of a new language, complete with a new grammar: a language that would answer the cannons of rationalism. The formal images produced by the machine and industrial methods of production provided the vocabulary.

Industrialization, however, meant not only a new formal language borne out of industrial processes, but also the introduction of a whole new set of conceptual images and a new attitude toward the places of man. This included concepts such as "standardization," "beneficial concentration," "mass production", "modular components," etc.

The prime criterion of industrial processes, efficiency, penetrated architectural thinking and became a powerful tool in making architecture available to the new clientele. However, efficiency and optimization have only a utilitarian value; and standardization and modular coordination of components are a result not only of the mass production inherent in industrialization, but also of an attitude, equally inherent, which equates order with unity of style.

Industrial method is essentially a process involving a) analysis of the nature of components, and b) their synthesis into a problem solving the whole. This process,

appropriate as it is to problem-solving, has only a limited role in architecture. There is no human activity, including that of the architect, in which every component can be subjected to rational analysis. Nor can they all be reduced to simple, Newtonian categories.

It is obvious, therefore, that if the rationalistic approaches displayed basic indifference to those emotions and contradictions which, once admitted, would reveal human nature and its frailties, it is only because the limitations of the method — chosen a priori — limited their range of perception.

This is inevitable where "method" is understood to be an independent, free-standing concept. The limitations of the instruments of observation and communication limit the phenomena which we can observe or communicate. We have, therefore, been urged to look for the content of architecture outside of human nature, where it supposedly has an existence independent of human phenomena.

The above has necessarily been a brief outline of the major developments in modern architecture. These developments have not only shaped contemporary architecture but have formed our intellectual environment. It is against this background that we view the work of Kahn.

If rationalism and formalism were fundamentally indifferent to the circumstantial aspects of reality, the work of Kahn begins by recognizing those aspects. To be sure, he is neither the first nor the only man to have done so — James Joyce, Thomas Mann, Bergson and Schopenhauer all challenged the claim of reason as the supreme human value. But architecture fell behind developments in other fields, primarily for want of a vocabulary that could translate the unmeasurable world of the psyche into the measurable world of buildings. Louis Kahn sought to develop such a vocabulary.

Art is, by its very nature, ambivalent; only so can it express the dynamics of life and reality. The rationalistic view of reality is deterministic and is based on a world of objects in which form and shape are indistinguishable, interchangeable concepts. This view of reality does not admit ambivalence. Instead of resolving the tension between the universal and the particular in a way that will express this ambivalence, the problem itself is often ignored. The reality of Louis Kahn, as he expressed it in his distinction between form and shape, exists at once on the universal and on the particular levels; the universal, instead of being taken for granted as an abstract entity existing outside of human phenomena, is constantly being tested and reaffirmed by the particular.

The "form" of the building comes from realizing the inherent nature of the institution which demands presence. "Form" is universal in the sense that there is an inevitability to its realization and that the possibility of such realization is common to all men. The "shape," on the other hand, is a product of an intensely creative act which transforms the universal by subjecting it to trial by circumstances. The building, therefore, is an affirmation of the multiplicity of life.

An important element of Kahn's thought is his conception of man. The validity of architecture lies not only in what a building looks like, or how well it performs, or what symbols it articulates, but also in what life it addresses itself to. After all is said and seen, one will remember Frank Lloyd Wright, Gropius, Corbusier or Boullée for the vision of life and man they pursued throughout their creative career.

Kahn's view of man suggests that man is neither rational nor irrational but, for lack of a better word, "integrated." In order to view man thus in his totality, it is necessary that he be freed from determinism and the principle of causality with which we view nature and to which natural phenomena are subjected. The dangers of viewing man on the model of nature have become obvious in the past few decades; these dangers stem from the fact that man, thus modeled, is only partial man.

Kahn's assertion that man is not nature but is made by nature forces a re-evaluation of our concept of man. He sees the man/nature dichotomy at once on two levels: man the species and man the human. Though made out of the substances of nature and being subject to the laws of nature, the human psyche has a reality essentially independent of nature, though not necessarily antagonistic to it. This non-antagonistic relationship between man and nature is in direct contrast to the view which sees this relationship as essentially that of control of one by the other. It is non-antagonistic because it strives toward an ultimate unity of man and nature based not on sameness of form but achieved only through the creative act of man, which requires a sympathetic appreciation of nature and its active participation.

This reciprocity of perspective in which man and world mirror each other demands a certain structure of constants in human nature and, by implication, a re-evaluation of the concept of history, since history, with evolution as its theme, has left man devoid of any constants and prerequisite attributes. History, by attempting to arrange the apparent variables of cultural diversity in a temporal and evolutionary frame, has sought to explain away this diversity as mere stages of human evolution.

Traditionally, the direction of history has been from primitive to civilized man, which is to say from pre-rational to rational man. It is evident that history has been used by rationalists to construct a philosophical system justifying reason as the supreme value and goal.

Whether one views history as dialectical or analytical, we have no choice, as Levi-Strauss has pointed out, but to see it as a process of evolution. The only way to get around this dilemma without negating history altogether is by limiting the ties between history and man to the extent that history is an indispensable tool in cataloging the elements of any structure, human or non-human.

The answer, then, regarding the essential nature of man lies not in the course of history but, rather, in the beginning. Kahn has expressed his perception of this eloquently: "It is my desire to sense Volume Zero. Volume minus one. A search for the sense of beginning, because I know that the beginning is an eternal confirmation. I say eternal because I distinguish it from, let's say, universal. 'Universal' deals with the laws of nature and 'eternal' deals with the nature of man."

The two concepts most prevalent in Kahn's thought are *order* and *validity*. Kahn suggests that even though order is a precondition of all existence, architecture is concerned with more than merely duplicating the harmonious relationships — always present in nature — between objects. The order of human endeavors is linked to the consciousness of man: "Nature does not do things consciously, while man does." Order, then, is a "level of creative consciousness, forever seeking a higher level". Consciousness is defined as a totality of man's thought and feeling. The higher the level of integration between thought and feeling, the higher the level of order. This integration, in turn, leads to the realization of what Kahn calls the "existence will" of a particular architectural element — what it wants to be or what its essential nature is.

Architecture has always sought to relate to nature by mirroring the sublime qualities of nature. The relationship between architecture and man, on the other hand, has always been more elusive; at the most, it has remained at the utilitarian level. The terms "designing for man" or "humane architecture" have proven to be good revolutionary slogans but not much else. The intense identification between man and architecture demanded by Kahn as a prerequisite for the realization of architecture's essential nature makes it necessary to consider that relationship anew. It also calls for a fundamental re-evaluation of the problem of form, content, and structure.

Like order, Kahn's "validity" is also an extension of the man/nature duality: Nothing in nature comes into existence and is sustained unless it has validity: a purpose and a place. This is physical validity. It is built around and controlled by the laws of nature, which are universal. The validity of the work of man, on the other hand, is fundamentally different from, but not necessarily antagonistic to, physical validity; in fact, architecture belongs to that in-between zone where this duality finds a resolution. It is where the universal and the eternal coexist.

The term "validity" as used by Kahn is, in fact, very close to his concept of truth. This may seem strange to us, since in the Western intellectual tradition validity implies only relative truth — that which is relevant in a particular situation. In a culture that has articulated the universal patterns of thinking, the distinction between cognition (which can be justified by the application of universal rules of logic) and relevance (which cannot be justified without relying on tradition and cultural criteria) is inevitable. However, if cognition and relevance are not interchangeable, the relationship between truth and validity — which they have come to imply — is altogether different. Truth and validity are not opposed to each other; in fact, truth is the very essence of validity. To say that truth is based on reason and is, therefore, universal, while validity is based on spatial, temporal, and cultural circumstances, is bound to lead one to a dilemma of commitment.

Relevance has become a magic word for architects. It implies a certain urgency to belong. This is only another form of the concern for civic accountability. However, forcing a choice between truth and relevance limits the very purpose and content of architecture. By preferring the term "validity" over relevance and by distinguishing among physical, psychological, and spatial validities, Kahn has come closest to resolving this dilemma.

His reasoning is fundamental rather than historical; his discoveries of new forms of expression are based on the inherent validities of such forms rather than on our immediate needs for them. There are no such things as "modern" materials or "modern" architecture; the spirit of architecture, like the spirit of poetry, transcends time and history. The clue to that spirit resides in the eternal beginning, when the demands for presence meet the instruments of expression.

Architecture is an idea; its constituent elements are the institutions it serves. A building has not only a unique organization of institutions but also a unique conception of "organization" itself. Every spatial element in Kahn's buildings is dedicated to an institution. It is in this "making of a room" that the essence of his architecture becomes evident: the "room" derives its appropriateness — its size, shape, light, etc. — from the nature of the institution it serves, and its architecture evokes in us a sense of the beginning of that institution. Kahn's concern for the identity and integrity of these "rooms" is manifest in the composition of the buildings. The apparent discontinuities and articulateness in the plan form are the result of a desire not to compromise the integrity of any of these elements. The continuities come from the way the elements relate with each other through an idea.

The personal character of Kahn's vocabulary manifests itself in the fact that his philosophy is not a simple and direct extension of the architectural thought that has dominated the larger part of modern history. Kahn seeks to go beyond history, to the beginning, in search of an entirely new set of conceptual images that will better suit his sense of reality, and for which the present vocabulary is insufficient. His work, therefore, besides being highly personal and deeply felt, involves a fundamental re-evaluation of the nature and purpose of architecture.

The city, from a simple settlement, became the place of the assembled institutions. Before, the institution was the natural agreement — the sense of commonality. The constant play of circumstances, from moment to moment unpredictible, distort inspired beginnings of natural agreement.

The measure of greatness of a place to live must come from the character of its institutions, sanctioned through how sensitive they are to renewed agreement and desire for new agreement, not through need, because it comes from what already is. Desire is the jet not yet made — the roots of the will to live.

The City from a simple settlement became the place of the assembled Institutions

A mere foothold is confident of the settlement—The first Institution.

Before the Institution was natural agreement—the sense of commonality. The constant play of circumstances, from moment to moment unpredictable distort Inspiring beginnings of natural agreement.

The measure of the greatness of a place to live must come from the character of its Institutions sanctioned thru how sensitive they are to renewed. and Desire for new Agreement

(not need because it comes from us; Desire is the jet not made the roots of the will to live)

The City

1 Plan for the Center of Philadelphia

2 Bicentennial Exposition
Philadelphia, Pennsylvania

3 Abbasabad Development Project
Teheran, Iran

1 Plan for the Center of Philadelphia

Project 1956–1962

In 1956, while acting as a consultant to the Philadelphia Planning Commission, Kahn developed a comprehensive scheme for vehicular and pedestrian movement in the heart of Philadelphia.

Kahn felt that, instead of taking corrective action, streets needed to be redefined in view of automobile traffic.

In his schemes, streets were conceived as rivers and canals, parking became harbors or docks, while several streets were freed of auto traffic and given back to pedestrians.

Diagram of existing movement.

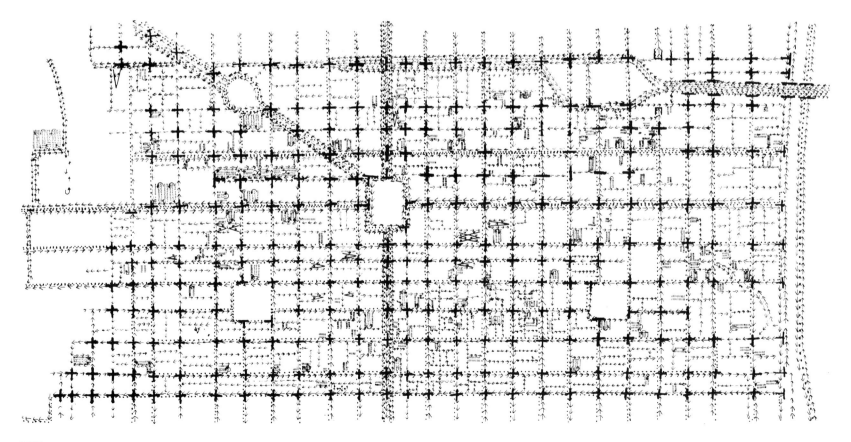

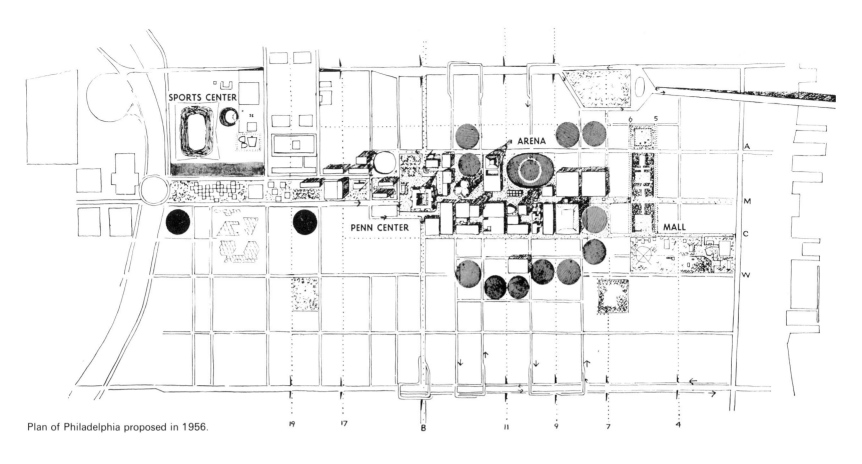

Plan of Philadelphia proposed in 1956.

Diagram of proposed movement.

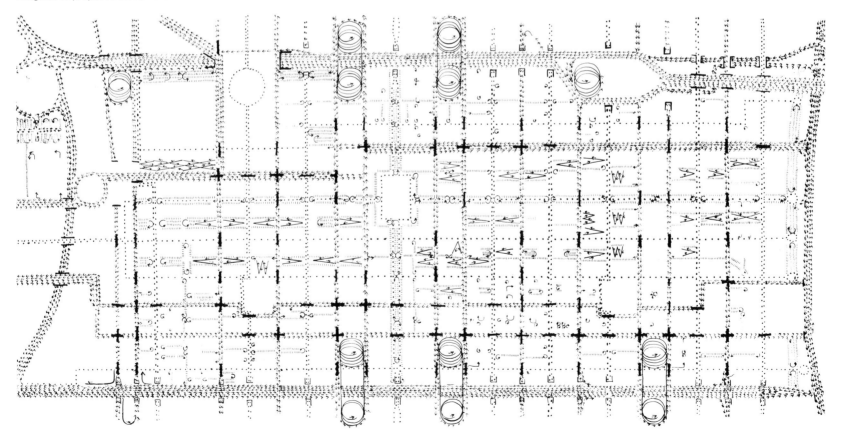

227

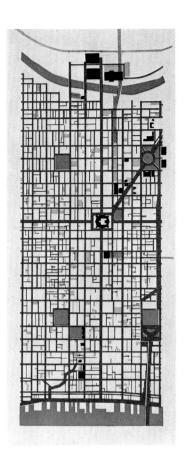 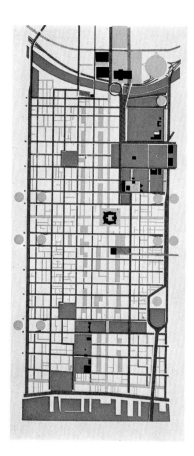 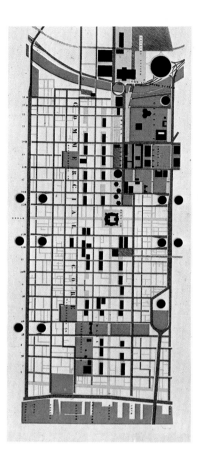

Streets are now used indiscriminately for all purposes and varieties of movement. It is intended by this plan to *re-define the use of streets* and separate one type of movement from another so that cars, buses, trolleys, trucks and pedestrians will move and stop more freely, and not get in each other's way.

This plan is based on a concept of *street design* analagous to a system of waterways, of rivers and canals with wharfs and docks for stopping.

Flow streets — rivers or expressways (red) as a part of their design are provided with wharfs in the form of free or low cost Municipal Garages for all day use of cars and within reasonable walking distance of offices.

Go streets — or canals (brown) afford access to the center city, free of trolleys, local buses and parked vehicles and with a reduced number of intersections.

Stop streets — or dock streets (yellow), blocked from uninterested through traffic, for staccato movement of trolleys, local buses, parking and service.

Docks — (yellow) space for deliveries and loading, for parking, service stations and short time commercial parking garages. Existing minor streets, increased where needed, are zoned for these purposes and blocked to through traffic. Many parking garages now existing are located in suggested dock areas.

Pedestrian ways — (green) are primarily shopping streets unharassed by cars and trucks allowing the movement of trolleys or local buses for the convenience of shoppers and office workers.

This system of movement through the center city area is not designed for speed but for order and convenience. The present mixture of staccato, through, stop and go traffic makes all the streets equally ineffectual. The orderly discrimination of traffic of varying intentions should tend to facilitate flow and thereby encourage rather than discourage entrance of private cars into the center of town.

It is further intended by this system to stimulate more imaginative development of our shopping areas along the lines of the new suburban shopping centers which provide for a similar pattern of movement for pedestrian and motor. This distinction of types of movement could also give rise to new building and merchandising ideas. Chestnut Street as a pedestrian street with a single trolley line becomes in a sense a 60 foot sidewalk. Trees could be planted or shelters built for shade, and the sidewalk cafe will most likely appear.

The *commercial core* — is accentuated in this study for the purpose of suggesting that the contemplated development of the Chinese Wall-Pennsylvania Boulevard area should not be isolated from the Core. The strength of the new development lies in tying it together with existing shopping and commercial patterns.

The sunken *Mall* on the level of the pedestrian concourse as developed by Mr. Bacon is incorporated in the general scheme. It is suggested that the Mall be broadened in front of the tall Suburban Station Building to express the *suburban gateway*. New air conditioned office buildings along Market Street and Pennsylvania Boulevard are arranged in twin tower rhythm.

City Hall is obsolete and it is suggested that it be brought down except for the Tower (a suggestion developed by Paul Cret 25 years ago). The *Intercity Bus Station* is placed in this area at the intersection of the subways and between the Pennsylvania Suburban and Reading R.R. Stations to serve the department stores to the east and serve the developments of large single commercial operations to the west. The *New City Hall* including the courts and technical buildings is located in the Triangle Area as part of our enlarged *Civic and Cultural Center* at Logan Square. This move anticipates stimulation of developments westward and reclamation of the Schuylkill River for recreation. This relatively inexpensive area would allow for the continued development of the expanding functions of our city government and would eventually reveal itself as the new Philadelphia Landmark — an impressive entrance to the center city at its rail and motor gateway.

Over part of the railroad yards of the 30th Street Station, a *Transportation Gateway* is proposed, tying together two levels of passenger tracks, the high level freight line, a trucking level and a helicopter air connection as a transportation interchange and a freight center. This would consolidate some of the services of the Pennsylvania Railroad now spread over a large area, and serve the needs of the Post Office and the new Bulletin building.

In this approach to re-planning the center city by re-definition and design of the street, the forms of its wharf and dock buildings strategically located as a part of the flow pattern predict the beginnings of a new urban sculpture of a city designed for movement.

Expressways are like RIVERS
These RIVERS frame the area to be served
RIVERS have HARBORS
HARBORS are the municipal parking towers
from the HARBORS branch a system of CANALS that serve the interior
the CANALS are the go streets
from the CANALS branch cul-de-sac DOCKS
the DOCKS serve as entrance halls to the building

"In Gothic times, architects built in solid stones. Now we can build with hollow stones. The spaces defined by the members of a structure are as important as the members. These spaces range in scale from the voids of an insulation panel, voids for air, lighting, and heat to circulate, to spaces big enough to walk through or live in.

The desire to express voids positively in the design of structure is evidenced by the growing interest and work in the development of space frames. The forms being experimented with come from a closer knowledge of nature and the outgrowth of the constant search for order. Design habits leading to the concealment of structure have no place in this implied order. Such habits retard the development of an art. I believe that in architecture, as in all art, the artist instinctively keeps the marks which reveal how a thing was done. The feeling that our present-day architecture needs embellishment stems in part from our tendency to fair joints out of sight, to conceal how parts are put together. Structures should be devised which can harbor the mechanical needs of rooms and spaces. Ceilings with structure furred in tend to erase scale. If we were to train ourselves to draw as we build, from the bottom up, when we do, stopping our pencil to make a mark at the joints of pouring or erecting, ornament would grow out of our love for the expression of method. It would follow that the pasting over the construction of lighting and acoustical material, the burying of tortured, unwanted ducts, conduits, and pipe lines, would become intolerable. The desire to express how it is done would filter through the entire society of building, to architect, engineer, builder, and craftsman."

Study sketch.

The new city center.

231

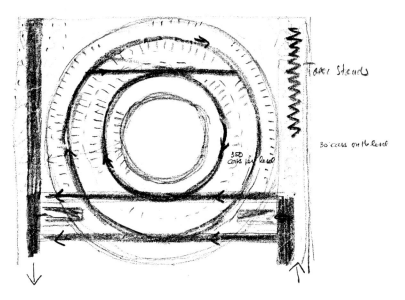

Sketch plan of Garage and Service Building.

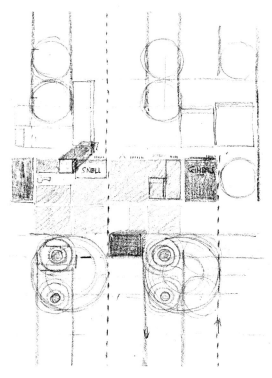

Sketch plan of center city.

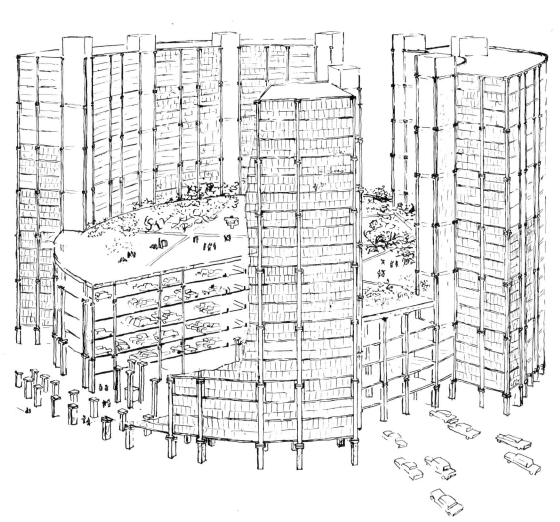

Kahn believes that a city has to be evaluated on the basis of its utility. When he worked out the traffic planning system for Philadelphia, he considered the streets as being equivalent to rivers, with docks, piers, and loading facilities. With this in mind, he designed his garages in the shape of stadiums, the outer faces of which were to accommodate flats and working premises. In this way, Kahn created stations that are organically in the general traffic movement.

In 1961, a Graham Foundation grant made it possible for Kahn to carry forward his vision for the center city first expressed in his traffic plan. The new plan consolidated various activities of the city such as government institutions, commercial, transportation, sports complex, etc. within the heart of the city. This complex was defined by a system of "viaducts," an architecture of movement. At selected locations "gates" were placed allowing entry into the center.

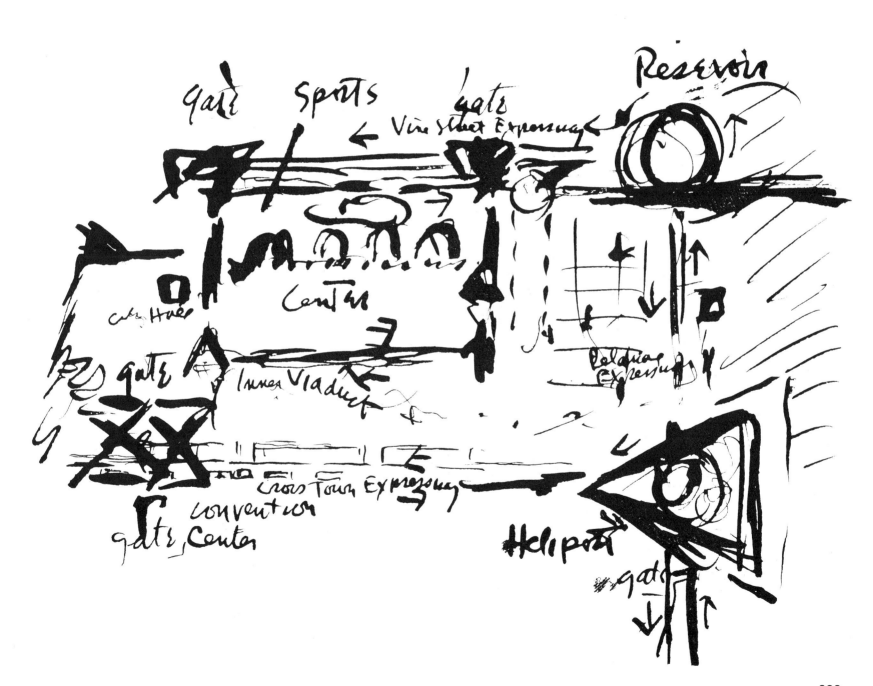

View looking north.

Sketch plan drawn over the existing map of Philadelphia.

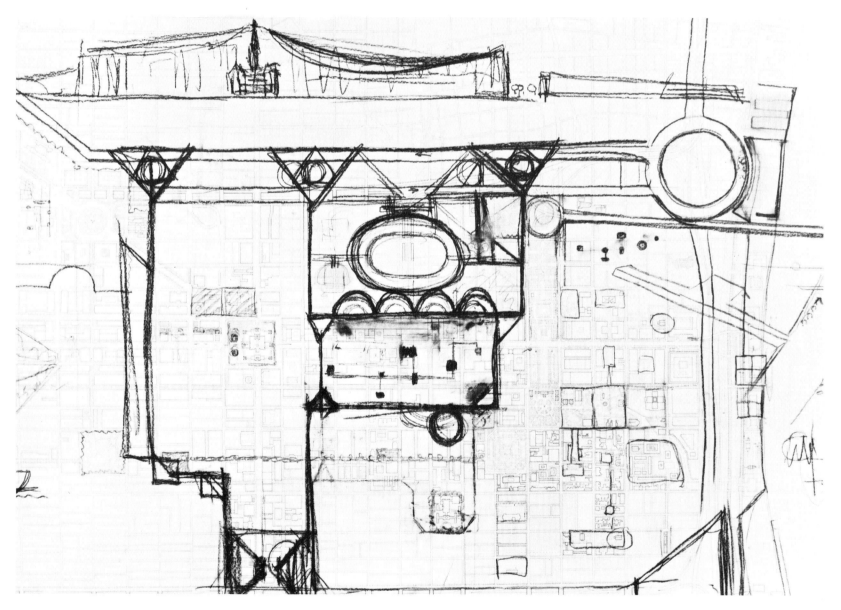

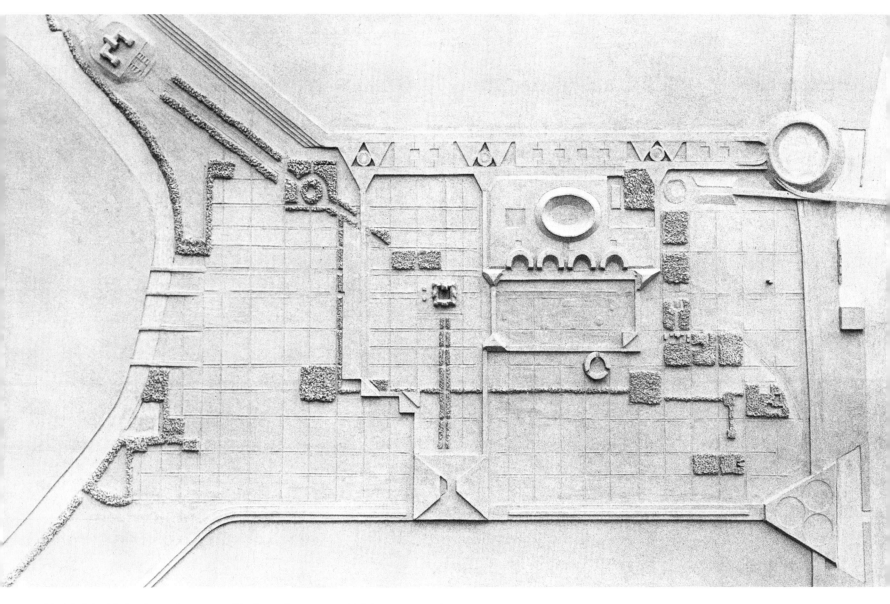

Model of the Market Street city center, with elevated motorways, highrise garages and semi-cylindrical office buildings.

Section through center city.

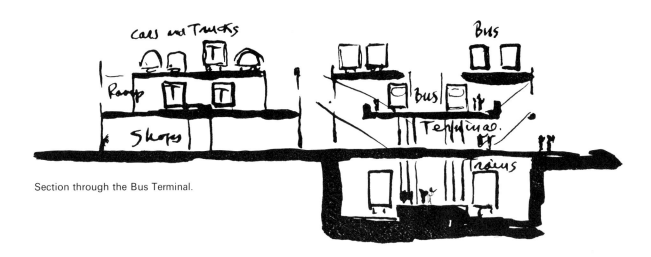

Section through the Bus Terminal.

Plan and elevation of Bus Terminal.

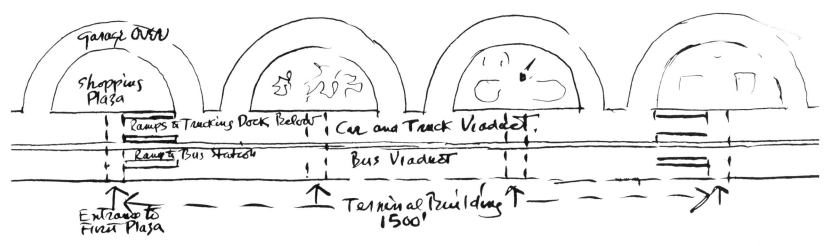

In 1957, the Concrete Institute of America commissioned Kahn to prepare a study for a high-rise tower built with concrete. The tower, which is 616 feet high, contains 3,000,000 square feet of work area. The structure is a vacuum precast, prestressed concrete triangulated strut frame, integrally braced by the cross framing and intersecting of the column system at 66 foot levels. Each intersection is crowned by a capital 11 feet deep, in which are housed storage, toilets, and sub-stations for mechanical services. Columns are hollow and contain conduits and pipes. Each 66-foot level is a structural floor. The floor-to-ceiling height of the intermediate floors may be varied to suit planning and vertical requirements. Floors are not directly over each other but shift in a triangular relationship to the natural geometric growth of the structure.

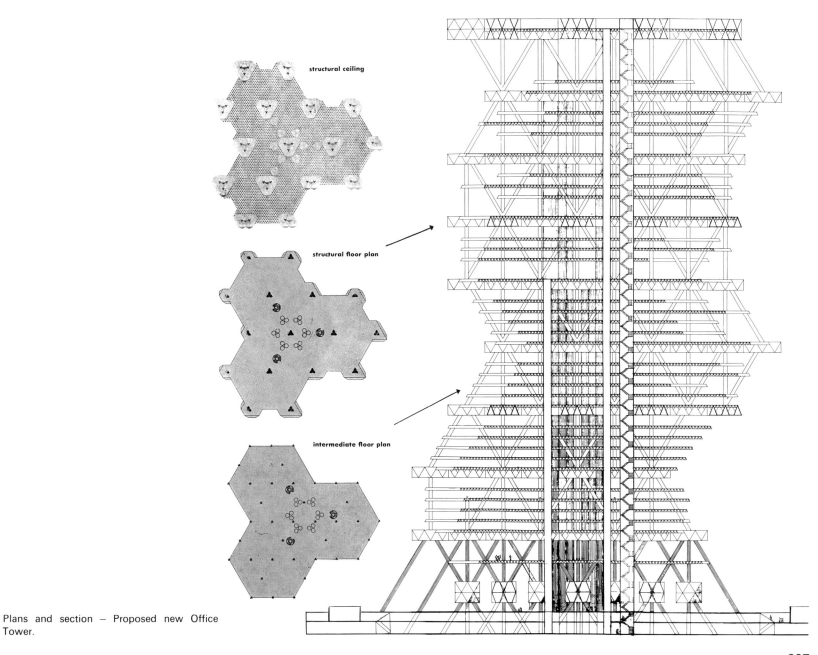

structural ceiling

structural floor plan

intermediate floor plan

Plans and section — Proposed new Office Tower.

The 700 by 700 foot square base of the tower is composed of three levels: 1) A shopping concourse at street level, 2) A pedestrian plaza one level above the street, and 3) A lower parking and service level. Entrance to parking is ramped around two diagonally opposite, 80 foot in diameter openings, which also bring natural light and air to the lowest level. The two remaining corners are designed for off-street docking of buses and taxis. On each side of the plaza are three additional, smaller air shafts surrounded by 80 by 80 foot square pedestrian entrance courts, which are lined with shops and give direct access to the mid-level shopping concourse. Escalators carry pedestrians to and from the lower parking level; stairs lead to the upper level.

1 View of the plaza.
2 Model – New Office Tower.

1

The Bicentennial on the Delaware

The American Building is an enclosed STREET several thousand feet long offered to all Nations for their expressions. It is the place of the inspired addenda coming from children and adults invited to formulate plans to bring new availabilities to all people. This crystal-like building of Invitation would present a simple image, inside of which would be the place of happening and a variety of structures tied to ordered services.

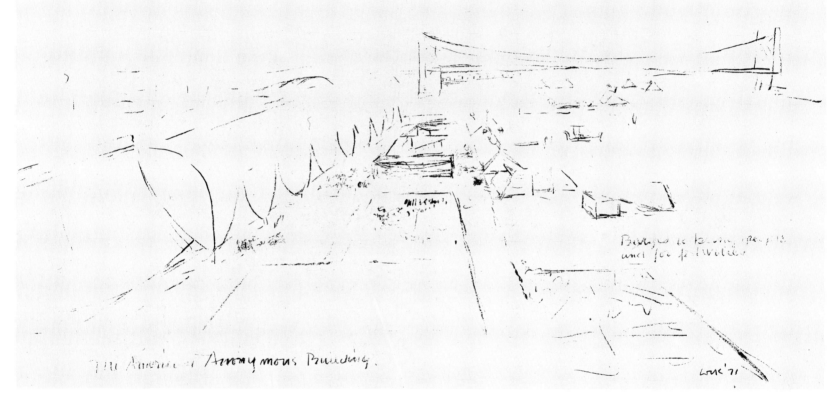

The Bicentennial in Delaware. The American Building is an enclosed street several thousand feet long, offered to all nations for their expressions. It is the place of the inspired addenda coming from children and adults invited to formulate plans to bring new availabilities to all people.
This crystal-like building of invitation would present a simple image, inside of which would be the place of happening and a variety of structures tied to ordered services.

2 Bicentennial Exposition Philadelphia, Pennsylvania

1971–1973

Louis Kahn was always fascinated by the idea of the American revolution. He took the opportunity of the Bicentennial celebration of American independence to express his interpretation of this revolution.

In 1971, Kahn proposed a plan for the western bank of the Delaware River. In 1972, a team of distinguished architects of Philadelphia was established under his leadership to prepare the plan for the celebration. The site was chosen near the airport.

Like the earlier plan on the Delaware River, this plan was also structured by a "street," on which each nation would have its house. This "street" was conceived as a threshold between expression and resources, silence and light.

Louis Kahn's plan for the Bicentennial Exposition in Philadelphia.

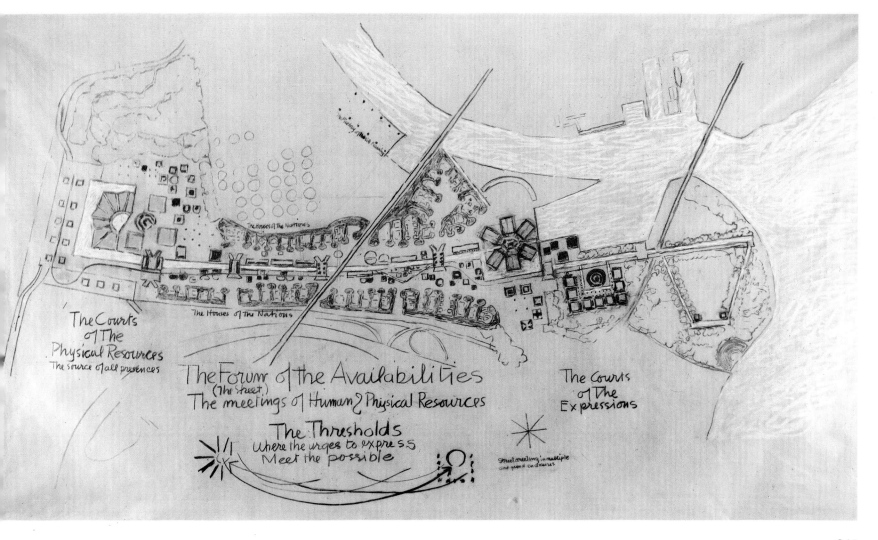

The Courts of The Physical Resources
The source of all presences

The Forum of the Availabilities
(The Street)
The meetings of Human & Physical Resources

The Thresholds
Where the urges to express
Meet the possible

The Courts of The Expressions

3 Abbasabad Development Project Teheran, Iran

Project 1974

A new civic and administrative center of Teheran is to be located among the hills of the Abbasabad district. Louis Kahn and Kenzo Tange were asked to make a joint proposal. This was the last project Louis Kahn worked on. The model shows the first composition. The commercial and business center (in triangular configuration) is flanked on one side by the sports complex, the municipal building, and the cultural and religious institutions, such as the university, art and science museums, and the mosque. The government offices are located on the other side of the mall.

This scheme was later extended towards the hills as a linear development, as shown in the sketch. The institutions and the sports complex have been moved to the hills. Here, Kahn conceived a "place of civic and natural meeting in regard to the way of life," very much like the Congress Hall in Venice. The hills surrounding this will accommodate the residential development.

Model of the first scheme.

Sketch of the second scheme. It is now extended among the hills. Kahn proposed an institution, similar to the Congress Hall in Venice, in the center.

The Architect as a Person

The work of a man is often discussed, analyzed, and studied as the manifestation of a general will. This is particularly true in architecture, which, being eventually considered the tangible evidence of a relationship between events and elements, rests fundamentally on the general aspiration of people to express.

Thus, those aspects of man's work which reveal an interpretation of issues, a way of approaching them, and the resolution of them into particular expression become of interest in exploring a general will.

However, in the study of the work of an artist, two interpretations usually emerge: one in which he is seen as capable of shaping that will, and the other whereby he becomes the catalyzer of that will.

The acceptance of either one of these interpretations becomes less and less appropriate when his work is no longer taken as the synthesis of a historical process but simply as the consequence of a human force, conscious of its own intentions.

Much of great architecture is the result of this consequence. The real contact with architecture and with the architect is made, then, beyond learned expressions of styles, when the substance of man's existence as an individual and as a community is simply but uncompromisingly stated.

This does not occur simply because a formal synthesis is obtained, but, rather, because a comprehensive idea of order is validated.

At its worst, today's world seems to be a world in which people are intent on setting their own rules. At its best, it is a world in which the discrepancies, the paradoxes, and the rejections represent a way of relating oneself to events and, in doing so, acquiring an awareness of the multiple aspects of life.

Today's artist, as a consequence, is bound to the destiny of his society and its institutions, even though he may at times appear as an individual enjoying what may be only an illusory freedom. His role is in living the process of events and taking upon himself the great risk of realizing the conjectures and the possibilities of that society: in particular, realizing the link between the infinite of nature and the finite of man.

Thus, he is a person willing and capable of taking that risk for a better and more conscious world, fully knowing that its future is not attained lying in the sun. It must be painstakingly built upon the present.

Louis Kahn was such a person. He assumed those risks as an artist and as an architect, concluding the work of at least two generations and setting the stage for work in the future. It was an all-encompassing risk, one "touching upon hope," as Dr. Eisely observed about the words of Francis Bacon — "We are not to imagine or suppose, but to discover what nature does or may be made to do."

Architects have been prone to elusive hopes. They have generally misjudged the course of events and presently are being treated with an insidious weariness caused by the repeated shattering of those hopes. They kept working for survival while man was searching for something more to live for; they expressed power and isolation but gradually lost their own freedom. "Necessity makes poor bargains" was a favorite remark of Benjamin Franklin, and Louis Kahn was found to repeat often to his young listeners, "Needs and wants produce little good; precious things come from aspiration and desire."

Louis Kahn's career was a continuous crisis, a testimonial to this continuous commitment. As a young boy he was once faced with the prospect of losing his eyesight. While walking home with a bag full of groceries he fell, hit his head on the pavement, and temporarily lost his vision. Within moments he decided that if he could not draw any more, he would be a musician.

"There is not the next building," he used to say. This implied that all his energies, his passion and wit were devoted to something at stake in a single issue that encompassed the whole of his artistic experience. This reflects not a personalistic attitude but, rather, a laborious, inexhaustible, painstaking search for identity for those rooms of which the building is made — identity with human issues — identity of himself as a person.

Thus, there seems to be a fundamental distinction between a personality and a person. A personality with related idiosyncracies is bent to shape events according to an interpretation that soon acquires its own alienated existence, losing meaning in direct proportion to its popularity.

A person is active, even if unconsciously, in the issues affecting his world, not by transposing those issues into theories, but by living them, acting in them, reacting to the human forces that generate them.

Thus, in architecture, conceptual structures, hypotheses, and models are elaborated through the screen of human participation. Directly or through his institutions, the architect will be selective in the process of reducing a general will into an abstract structure and then again into the original stuff, into a beginning. His work will never be the substitute for another thing. It will be the thing itself.

Louis Kahn, while being concerned with the things man has been looking for since the beginning — and in this he was a fundamentalist — was not interested in the realization of something which occurred already, but in the possibility that something will occur within the walls, spaces, and structures of his buildings, and probably because of them. This was his necessary condition for the presence of architecture.

At this point, it is important to follow briefly an itinerary of Louis Kahn's experiences, to review some aspects of his method, and finally, to relate his work to the current crisis of architecture.

Philadelphia is a town of domestic elegance — at least it was not too long ago — with well-calibrated streets and comfortable sidewalks, often lined with trees. In the suburbs, the trees actually make most of the architecture, hovering on the spirited language of the Victorian mansions or the plain stone surfaces of the Colonial. Germantown Avenue *is* a "street," winding up toward Chestnut Hill with a rhythmical sequence of well-built town houses.

The simple fabric of the 18th century town, resting between the gentle curves of two rivers, is given firm structure and focus by the location of the five squares of William Penn. This relatively static setting is dramatically cut by a deep diagonal, the Parkway, built in the 19th century, directly connecting the city with the country through Fairmount Park. Few cities are endowed with a more successful decision to link the urban with the country in one conscious gesture. As a result, the view upon entering the core of Philadelphia from the northwest is, indeed, like that of no other American city. This view is deep, carried by the diagonal into the center, firmly established by the bulk of City Hall.

For years, the aspirations of Louis Kahn were maturing

on this ground. A continuous exploration of the relationship between those rivers, those squares, streets, edges, and enclosures came to fruition in the plan for Philadelphia — an alternative for movement to the pivotal points of the city through viaducts, canals, parks, and the way in which they can enrich life. Previously in his work, this often resulted in formal solutions that made immediate contact between the core of a house and the outside, between a cluster of buildings and the landscape or other situations of the urban environment. A diagonal, such as in the Goldenberg house, cuts through the structure of a building spatially. In plan, it is a clear yet ambiguous gesture, as it suddenly introduces a relationship of complex definition. To the multiple parallel enclosures of a classical building and to the "plan libre" (two similar aspects of limit) Louis Kahn proposed an alternative, both spatial and compositional in the distribution of parts, which was to become a characteristic of so much of his work.

Inevitably, this touches the dilemma which persisted in the United States between two attitudes in architecture: the naturalization of spaces of Frank Lloyd Wright, and the cultural sophistication of Mies van der Rohe.

Perhaps neither one could really respond to the new crisis the American community was going to face with the aftermath of the Second World War — a crisis that would transform deeply the social and physical fabric of their cities and country.

Before and during the years of the depression, Louis Kahn worked in the office of Paul Cret, the Frenchman who designed the Parkway and the Museum; and later, the intellectual contacts he made in Philadelphia with George Howe, Oskar Stonorov, and Kenneth Day were significant, as was, more recently, the one with Robert Le Ricolais. George Howe left, besides the unique PSFS building, which he designed with Lescase, a number of town houses in a sophisticated, aristocratic version of the International Style. Oskar Stonorov, with his active social consciousness, could not fail to stimulate Kahn's interest in the human problems of large cities. These were the problems to which Louis Kahn reacted in a singular way by transforming the local and immediate issue into that of man's institution: an ideological place, but also a tangible entity in which people resolve individual aspirations to well-being. Thus, housing is not regarded as an emergency or transitional solution. It is an "assembly of rooms," intimate spaces for human activities. It is towers or town houses, never linear common "blocks" (clever arrangements of single or double-loaded corridors, a term Louis Kahn heartily despised). In the town houses of Philadelphia at 48th Street, the physically modest buildings convey a human scale through the precise figuration of entrance doors and window openings emphasized by large lintels.

Yet, if the major influence in Louis Kahn's experience may be the city and its life, there have been in his expressions repeated references to the natural background of the city, the parks, the rivers, the valleys, and the ancient trees of the country roads — references to that setting of the suburbs of Philadelphia where "the trees are the architecture of the street."

Several commissions outside the United States took Louis Kahn travelling and, although the contact with India and Bangladesh was prolonged and difficult, it was also an invaluable stimulus of ideas. He was capable of finding in India the same men with whom he had been working at home, his students as well as his colleagues. In an environment of different emphasis — emphasis that involved people and nature, ways of working, and attitudes — his eternal aspirations to a sense of life were renewed.

One is tempted to compare the Salk Institute with the Indian Institute of Management. Both projects are motivated by the same aspirations of man — science, learning, meeting, etc. — but their forms and expressions are different. At Salk, the poetic content reaches a particular lyricism expressing a relationship between culture and nature. The site plan, location of buildings and clusters, and the architecture of the laboratories possess the flexibility of being both neutral images and active concepts. The symmetry within an asymmetrical site, the contrasts between precise masses and the crumbling cliffs, and the attentive social significance given to each part of the complex produce a framework transforming the cultural values of science into the natural.

In India, the round forms, the circles of the arches, and the pointed brick walls merge the forms into a dense chromaticism of light and air. It is not a different climatic condition shaping those forms but a different pace of life, a different rapport of people with the earth, the rhythm of their thoughts and acts, to all of which Kahn became particularly sensitive after India. Thus the contact with India and Bangladesh was a new point of departure for Louis Kahn. His more recent projects in Venice, Jerusalem, and Baltimore are not the search for a universal language but for the settings for different cultures, and yet they are bent for things man has been searching for since the beginning.

Finally, this itinerary would not be complete without reference to Kahn as a teacher. It was here that he felt the ultimate freedom of the mind. Twice a week he looked forward to being with his students; young men and women from all over the globe made the studio at the University of Pennsylvania a place of encounter, a crossroad of minds, at once, both an idea and an institution. (The encounter was between the singularities.) It was a place not for instruction but to search for the agreement. "I felt most satisfied as a teacher only in those moments when I did not have to say 'This is how I would do it'." It was here that Kahn looked for and received the response and the confirmation of his beliefs. He conceived of the university as a place where freedom is achieved so that evaluation of the hypotheses and actions of life are possible. "The profession is in the market place — architecture belongs to the university."

"A person learns only that which is already within himself," Louis Kahn was fond of saying. Learning was, for him, a constant discovery of one's own self. "In man is the record of man, of what made him." Thus, the events, circumstances, and contacts in the life of Louis Kahn not only formulated his attitude toward the issues affecting our world, but also, and probably even more so, made him conscious of those forces which were already present within himself. Thus, he was a person, alone. Cutting through the dilemma of choice between Frank Lloyd Wright and Mies van der Rohe, he made a new beginning. He broke through the traditions of the Modern Movement in architecture and formulated a new platform with a new emphasis. The structural and functional correspondence between the spaces of human concern and the elements that serve them represented, at the same time, a body of theory and the plastic substance of a building. The Yale Art Gallery and the Trenton Community Center are historically the first buildings in which this was announced. It was more than a technical answer to a technical problem. It was a lesson that came in the midst of the "Brutalist" alternative, which began with Ronchamps, and of Mies van der Rohe's celebration of technology. It was as if Kahn sensed the beginning that was already in the air — a new culture, embryonic, erratic, and yet laboriously reaching for new values. "Today, even the sun is not being taken for granted," he once said.

List of Photographers

Dan Barberry 141, Cameraphoto Venice 160, 162 (2), George Cserna 30, 31, John Condax 207, John Ebstel 21 (4), 32, 39, 41, 92, 116, 181, 188 (27), 202, 205, Lionel Freedman 64, 65, Jaimini Mehta 21 (8, 9), 22, 23, 26, 43, 91, 122, 124, 211, Marshall Meyers 21 (5), 94, 97, 98, 188 (28), 201, National Design Institute, India 76 (Rohit Modi), 80 below, 83 (P.M. Dalwadi), George Pohl 44, 54, 56, 66, 89, 101, 117 (left and top right), 119 (above), 123, 150, 154, 159 (below), 162 (1), 167, 168, 170, 175, 176, 215, 242, Anant Raje 78, 79, 81, 84, 186, Marvin Rand 67, 72, 73, 74, Cervin Robinson 199, Ezra Stoller 21 (6, 7), Henry Wilcot 134, 139, 140, 145, 147, 149, Kurt Wyss 135.

Biography

Louis Isidore Kahn was born on February 20, 1901, on the Island of Osel, Estonia (Russia). His family emigrated to the United States in 1905. On the 17th of March, 1974, he died of a heart attack at Pennsylvania Station in New York on his way back from a trip to India.

He lived a rich and eventful life. The following is a brief account of his life as an architect and a teacher.

Education and Professional Career

1912–20	Central High School and the Pennsylvania Academy of Fine Arts. Received numerous prizes for drawing and painting
1920–24	University of Pennsylvania. Bachelor of Architecture
1925–26	Joined office of John Molitor. Became "Chief of Design" for Sesquicentennial Exposition
1928–29	Travelled in Europe
1932–33	Organizer and director of Architectural Research Group. Thirty unemployed architects and engineers studied Philadelphia housing conditions, planned housing projects, made city planning and slum clearance studies, investigated new construction methods, etc.
1930	Joined office of Paul P. Cret
1935	Registered with American Institute of Architects. Began independent practice
1937	Consultant Architect for the Philadelphia Housing Authority
1939	Consultant Architect for the U.S. Housing Authority
1941–42	Associated in practice with George Howe
1942–43	Associated in practice with George Howe and Oscar Stonorov
1946–52	Consultant architect for the Philadelphia City Planning Commission
1950–51	Resident architect – American Academy in Rome, Italy
1959	Delivered closing address, CIAM Tenth Congress, Otterlo, Holland
1960	Participated in World Design Conference, Tokyo, Japan
1961	Consultant Architect, Philadelphia City Planning Commission
1962	Delivered Annual Discourse to Royal Institute of British Architects, London, England
1968	Member, Philadelphia Fine Arts Commission

Academic Career

1947–57	Professor of Architecture, Yale University, Chief Critic of Architectural Design
1956	Albert Farwell Bennis Professor at School of Architecture and Planning, M.I.T.
1957	Professor of Architecture, University of Pennsylvania
1960	Lecturer at Yale, Harvard, University of California, University of Houston, University of North Carolina, Tulane University, Fellow at Princeton
1962	Lectured in Philadelphia, Ontario and Chicago
1966	Paul Philippe Cret Chair in Architecture, University of Pennsylvania
1971	Paul Philippe Cret Professor Emeritus, University of Pennsylvania

Honorary Degrees, Memberships and Fellowships

1964	Elected Member of National Institute of Arts and Letters
	Doctor of Architecture, Polytechnic Institute of Milan, Italy
	Doctor of Humanities, University of North Carolina
1965	Doctor of Fine Arts, Yale University
1966	Member of Royal Swedish Academy of Fine Arts
1967	Doctor of Laws, LaSalle College
	Member, College of Architects of Peru
1968	Fellow, American Academy of Arts and Sciences
	Doctor of Fine Arts, The Maryland Institute College of Art
1970	Fellow, American Institute of Architects
	Fellow, Royal Society of Arts, London, England
	Doctor of Fine Arts, Bard College

1971   Doctor of Fine Arts, University of Pennsylvania

1973   Member, American Academy of Arts and Letters

Exhibitions

1929–30   Exhibited paintings and drawings of European travels at Pennsylvania Academy of Fine Arts

1936   Museum of Modern Art, New York. Architecture in Government Housing

1963   Single Building Exhibition. "The Richards Medical Towers," Museum of Modern Art, New York

1965   La Jolla Museum of Art

1966   Retrospective Exhibition, Museum of Modern Art, New York

1968   Single Building Exhibition. "Palazzo dei Congressi," Venice, Italy

Awards and Recognitions

1960   Arnold Brunner Prize by The National Institute of Arts and Letters

1961   Fellowship for Advanced Studies in Fine Arts "to pursue his investigation of larger aspects of civic design," Graham Foundation

1962   Medal for Achievement – Philadelphia Art Alliance

1969   Silver Medal for Distinguished Contribution to the Arts – University of Connecticut
Gold Medal, Philadelphia Chapter of American Institute of Architects

1970   Gold Medal, New York Chapter of American Institute of Architects

1971   Gold Medal, American Institute of Architects

1972   Royal Gold Medal in Architecture, Royal Institute of British Architects, London, England

The House

1945–49   For Dr. and Mrs. Philip Q. Roche, Montgomery County, Pa.

1947–49   For Dr. and Mrs. Winslow Tompkins, Germantown, Pa. (Project)

1948–49   For Mr. and Mrs. Morton Weiss, Montgomery County, Pa.

1949   For Mr. and Mrs. Samuel Genel, Montgomery County, Pa.

1950   For Mr. and Mrs. Jacob Sherman, Montgomery County, Pa.

1952–53   Mill Creek Public Housing, Project I, Philadelphia, Pa.

1953   For Mr. and Mrs. Ralph Roberts, Germantown, Pa. (Project)

1954   For Dr. and Mrs. Francis Adler, Philadelphia, Pa. (Project)
For Mr. and Mrs. Weber DeVore, Montgomery County, Pa. (Project)

1957–59   Alterations and additions to residence of Irving L. and Dorothy E. Shaw. Philadelphia, Pa.

1957–61   For Mr. and Mrs. Fred E. Clever, Camden County, N.J.

1958   For Mr. Lawrence Morris, Mount Kisco, N.Y. (Project)

1959   For Mr. Robert H. Fleisher, Elkins Park, Pa. (Project)
For Mr. and Mrs. M. Morton Goldenberg, Rydal, Pa. (Project)

1959–61   For Dr. and Mrs. Bernard Shapiro, Narberth, Pa.
Residence for a single person, Chestnut Hill, Pa. (Esherick House)

1959–62   Mill Creek Housing Project II, Philadelphia, Pa.

1960–65   Eleanor Donnelly Erdman Hall, Dormitories, Bryn Mawr College, Pa.

1960   For Dr. and Mrs. Norman Fisher, Hatboro, Pa.

1966   Stern Residence, Washington, D.C.

Place of Worship

1954   Adath Jeshurun Synagogue, Elkins Park, Pa. (Project)

1959–67   First Unitarian Church, Rochester, N.Y.

1961–70   Mikveh Israel Synagogue, Philadelphia, Pa. (Project)

1965–68   Convent for the Dominican Sisters, Media, Pa. (Project)

1966   St. Andrew's Priory, California (Project)
Temple Beth El Synagogue, Chappaqua, N.Y.

1968   Hurva Synagogue, Jerusalem, Israel (Project)

Institutions

1951–53   Yale University Art Gallery, New Haven, Connecticut

1955–57   R.I.A.S. Research Institution for Advanced Study, Glenn L. Martin Company, Fort Mead, Md. (Project)

1956   Library, Washington University, St. Louis, Mo. (Competition Entry)

1959–65   Salk Institute for Biological Studies, La Jolla, Cal.

1960   Bristol Township Municipal Building, Levittown, Pa. (Project)
Chemistry Building, University of Virginia, Charlottsville, Va. (Project)
Shapero Hall of Pharmacy, Wayne State University, Detroit, Mich. (Project)

1963   Indian Institute of Management, Ahmedabad, India

1964   Hall of Ocean Life for the Peabody Museum of Natural History, Yale University, New Haven, Conn. (Project)

1964–67   Philadelphia College of Art, Philadelphia, Pa. (Project)

1967–72   Kimbell Museum of Art, Fort Worth, Texas

1967–72   Library and Dining Hall, Philip Exeter Academy, Exeter, N.H.

1968   Wolfson Center for Mechanical and Transportation Engineering, University of Tel-Aviv, Israel

1969   The Yale Center for British Art and British Studies, New Haven, Conn.

1973   Theological Seminary Library, University of California, Berkeley, Cal. (Project)

Place of Well-Being

1948   Jefferson National Expansion Memorial, St. Louis (Competition Entry)

1949–50   Occupational Therapy Building, Philadelphia Psychiatric Hospital, Philadelphia, Pa.

1950   Alteration to St. Luke's Hospital, Philadelphia, Pa.
Samuel Radbill Building, Philadelphia, Psychiatric Hospital, Philadelphia, Pa.

1954–59   Trenton Jewish Community Center, Trenton, N.J. (Project)

1955–56   Bath House, Trenton, N.J.

1956–57   Enrico Fermi Memorial Competition, Chicago, Ill. (Competition Entry)

1960–61   Franklin Delano Roosevelt Memorial Competition, Washington, D.C. (Competition entry)

1961   Barge on the Thames, England for American Wind Symphony
Plymouth Swim Club, Plymouth Township, Pa. (Project)
General Motors Exhibition, 1964 World's Fair, New York (Project)
United Neighborhood Playground, New York, N.Y. (with Isamu Noguchi)

1961–64   Fine Arts Building, Fort Wayne, Indiana (Project)

1962   Second Capitol of Pakistan, Dacca, East Pakistan (Bangladesh)

1963   Ayub Central Hospital and School of Tropical Medicine and Public Health, Dacca, East Pakistan (Bangladesh)

1964–67   "Interama," Inter-American Community, Miami, Florida (Project)

1965   Theater and Art School, Fort Wayne Foundation, Fort Wayne, Indiana
President's Estate, Islamabad, West Pakistan

1967–69   Memorial to Six Million Jews, Battery Park, N.Y. (project)

251

The Delaware Valley Mental Health Foundation, New Britain, Pa. (Poject)

1969 Congress Hall, Venice, Italy (Project)

1970 Family Planning Center, Kathmandu, Nepal

1971–73 Inner Harbor Development, Baltimore, Md. (Project)

1972 Government Hill Development, Jerusalem, Israel (Project)

1973 Franklin Delano Roosevelt Memorial, Roosevelt Island, N.Y.
Pocono Art Center, Pennsylvania (Project)
New Secretariat for the Capitol of Bangladesh, Dacca, Bangladesh

Place of Work

1948 Interior alterations to Radbill Oil Company, Philadelphia, Pa.

1954–56 American Federation of Labor Medical Service Plan Building, Philadelphia, Pa. (Demolished, 1973)

1957–61 Alfred Newton Richards Medical Research Building, University of Pennsylvania, Philadelphia, Pa.

1957 Biology Building, University of Pennsylvania, Philadelphia, Pa.

1958–61 Tribune Review Publishing Company Building, Greenburg, Pa.

1959–61 U.S. Consulate Building for Angola, Luanda (Project)

1961 Carborundum Company, Niagara Falls, N.Y. Warehouse and Regional Sales Office, Atlanta, Ga. and Mountainview, Cal. (Project)

1966–70 Factory Building, Olivetti-Underwood Corporation, Harrisburg, Pa.

1966–73 Office Building, Kansas City (Project)

Architecture of City

1946–54 Triangle Area Report for Philadelphia City Planning Commission, Philadelphia, Pa.

1951 East Poplar Redevelopment Area Plan, Philadelphia, Pa. (with Day, McAllister and Tyng)

1951–53 Southwest Temple Redevelopment Area Plan, Philadelphia (with Day, McAllister and Tyng)

1956–57 Planning Studies of Penn Center and Midtown Traffic, Philadelphia, Pa. (Project)

1957 A City Tower, Studies for Concrete Institute (Anne Tyng Associate) (Project)

1961–62 Market Street East Redevelopment Studies for Graham Foundation (Project)

1963–64 Plan for Gandhinagar, Capitol for the State of Gujarat, India (Project)

1968–73 Hill Central Area Redevelopment, New Haven, Conn. (Project)

1974 Abbasabad Redevelopment Project, Teheran, Iran. In Association with Kenzo Tange (Project)